CW01497249

THE ARCHAEOLOGY OF IRONBRIDGE GORGE IN 20 DIGS

Michael Nevell

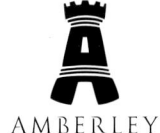

AMBERLEY

First published 2023

Amberley Publishing
The Hill, Stroud
Gloucestershire, GL5 4EP

www.amberley-books.com

Copyright © Michael Nevell, 2023

The right of Michael Nevell to be identified as the Author
of this work has been asserted in accordance with the
Copyrights, Designs and Patents Act 1988.

All rights reserved. No part of this book may be reprinted
or reproduced or utilised in any form or by any electronic,
mechanical or other means, now known or hereafter invented, including photocopying and recording,
or in any information
storage or retrieval system, without the permission in writing
from the Publishers.

British Library Cataloguing in Publication Data.
A catalogue record for this book is available from the British Library.

ISBN 978 1 3981 1156 1 (print)
ISBN 978 1 3981 1157 8 (ebook)

Typesetting by SJmagic DESIGN SERVICES, India.
Printed in Great Britain.

Contents

Introduction

'The iron bridge … is one of the wonders of the world'

John Byng, Viscount Torrington, 1784

Ironbridge is one of the birthplaces of global industrialisation, its name linked to both innovation and conservation. It has been regarded as a cradle of industry since the late eighteenth century, with the iconic Iron Bridge, manufactured by the Coalbrookdale Iron Company, becoming a tourist attraction as soon as it was built in 1779. However, industrial activity in the valley goes back much further. Abraham Darby's successful use of coke in 1709 to fuel a blast furnace originally built in

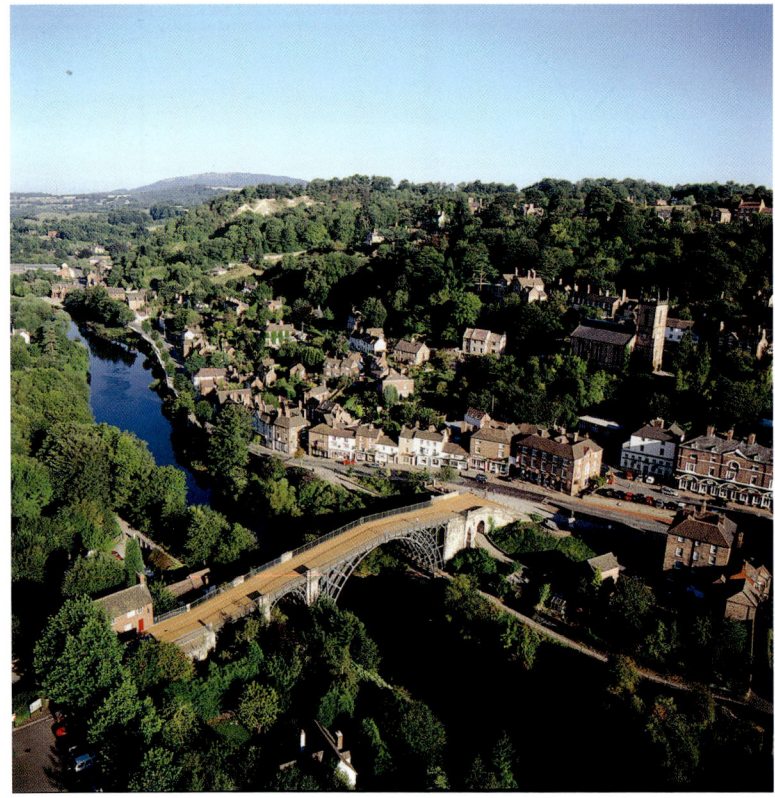

The 1779 Iron Bridge in the Ironbridge Gorge. On the northern bank lies the Market Square with a church behind on the hill. The bridge is a Scheduled Ancient Monument, in the care of English Heritage, and lies at the heart of the Ironbridge Gorge World Heritage Site. (© Ironbridge Gorge Museum Trust)

1658 ushered in an era of vastly increased iron production. This technological leap built upon extensive seventeenth-century ironworking throughout the area by the Brook family amongst others, and paved the way for the innovations of William Reynolds in the late eighteenth century. Yet there is more to Coalbrookdale and the Severn Gorge than ironmaking and these heroic industrialists. Coal mining and pottery manufacture helped to create new industrial communities, and transport developments in river, rail, and canal all contributed to the valley's industrial strength during the seventeenth, eighteenth, and nineteenth centuries. Not only can the valley boast the first coke blast furnace and the first iron bridges of the industrial age, but also the first manufacture of cast-iron steam engine cylinders, the first mass-produced iron wheels, the first iron rails, and the first steam railway locomotive. The manufacturers in the valley also produced what was probably the first iron boat and used for the first time a Boulton & Watt steam engine to blow an iron blast furnace directly, thereby removing the need for them to be sited near a watercourse. The long-term impact and legacy of these innovations, based as they were around a carbon economy, remain highly relevant in the twenty-first century (Griffin, 2018, 1–20; Hayman & Horton, 1999, 9–15).

This tradition of innovation and its global impact would not have happened without a quirk of nature that exposed all the rocks and minerals necessary for ceramic and metal production in one accessible place. At the end of the last ice age, roughly 10,000 years ago, weaknesses in the local limestone provided an escape route for water

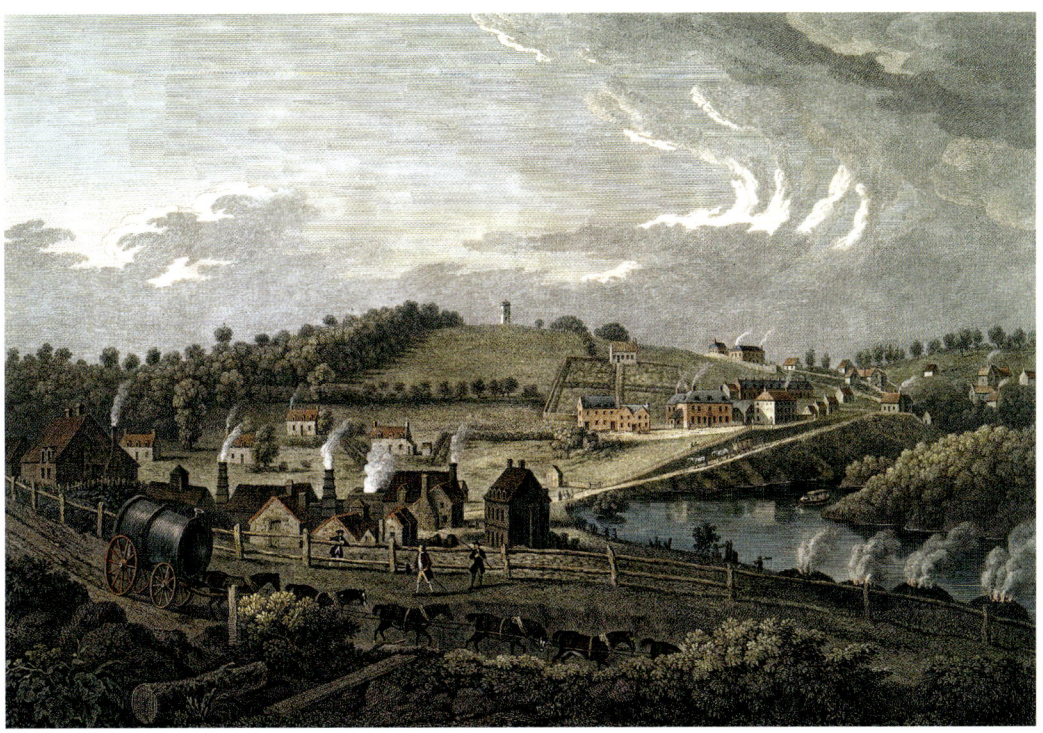

The earliest known engraving of industry in Coalbrookdale is this view of the Old Furnace and Upper Furnace Pool by Francois Vivares in 1758. (© Ironbridge Gorge Museum Trust)

trapped beneath an ice sheet to the north of Ironbridge. Under very high pressure this water carved out the steep-sided gorge seen in the twenty-first century. In the process this erosion exposed coal, clay, ironstone, limestone, and sandstone, enabling the late medieval and post-medieval growth of local industries that exploited these natural resources. The Coalbrookdale coalfield was mined from at least the fourteenth century, and by the seventeenth century the mining and export of coal from this area was of national importance and dominated the Gorge economy. The first blast furnaces in Shropshire were established in the 1550s and 1560s close to the Gorge, whilst the first mass steel production in Britain took place in Coalbrookdale from the 1610s to the 1680s (Belford & Ross, 2007; Belford, 2018, 137–144).

Limestone quarrying, iron ore mining and ironmaking, coal and clay mining, brick, ceramic, and tile manufacture all flourished during the seventeenth, eighteenth, and nineteenth centuries, and were of national and international significance in their technological impact (Brown, 1979, 160–168). The extensive transportation networks needed to move these raw materials to their production sites, and then to take the finished goods to market, were also nationally important in the development of the technology of industrial canals and railways, whilst Ironbridge built some of the earliest industrial communities to house the workers that kept these industries running. After the major industries declined in the early twentieth century, Ironbridge re-emerged as a centre for conservation and education around industrialisation, focussed upon the Ironbridge Gorge Museum Trust (IGMT), established in 1967. International recognition was formalised with the valley's inscription as a UNESCO World Heritage Site in 1986, whilst research and conservation of this international industrial legacy has continued into the twenty-first century (Clark & Alfrey, 1993; Hayman, Horton & White, 1999; Belford, Palmer & White, 2010; de Haan, 2011).

The UNESCO inscription for the Ironbridge Gorge World Heritage Site notes that 'The Industrial Revolution had its eighteenth-century roots in the Ironbridge Gorge and spread worldwide leading to some of the most far-reaching changes in human history'. This book looks at some of the key manufacturing, transport, and mining sites that helped to bring about this radical change in one West Midlands valley in England. Many of these industrial archaeology sites lie within the Ironbridge Gorge World Heritage Site and were recorded by IGMT's own archaeology unit. Archaeology is a bottom-up discipline, about individuals, their homes, and work life, and their interactions with the environment. Thus, the remains of everyday domestic and working life in Ironbridge, from bricks and cobbles to iron rails, ceramic vessels, and glass bottles, all help to bring to life this internationally important industrial landscape.

Ironbridge is often regarded as the spiritual home of British industrial archaeology, that branch of the discipline that deals with the archaeology of industrialisation, from manufacturing and extraction industries to transport infrastructure, factory workers' domestic dwellings, and the material culture of everyday lives in the eighteenth and nineteenth centuries. It was the site of one of the very first industrial museums in Britain, Abraham Darby's Old Furnace, opened in 1959, and has been the headquarters of the Association for Industrial Archaeology since it was formed in 1973. From the 1980s to the 2000s it led the way in industrial archaeology research through the Ironbridge Institute (founded in 1978) and the Ironbridge Archaeology Unit (established in 1981), helping to push the boundaries of the concept of industrial archaeology beyond the purely technical aspects of manufacturing and production synonymous with the Industrial Revolution (Belford, 2010a; Palmer, Nevell & Sissons, 2012, 1–2).

The selection of sites in the current volume is, inevitably, a personal choice, but I have endeavoured to show the reader how archaeology, the recovery of the physical remains of the human past, has contributed to our wider understanding of Ironbridge's industrial importance, and those who lived and worked in this landscape, since the first dig here in the 1960s. The chapters are arranged broadly in chronological order of investigation, with archaeological digs and surveys highlighting important industries, transport connections, and domestic sites. They also show how our understanding of Ironbridge's role in the industrialisation of Britain and beyond, the management and conservation of those sites, and the wider legacy of the first fossil-fuel-based Industrial Revolution, continues to evolve in the twenty-first century.

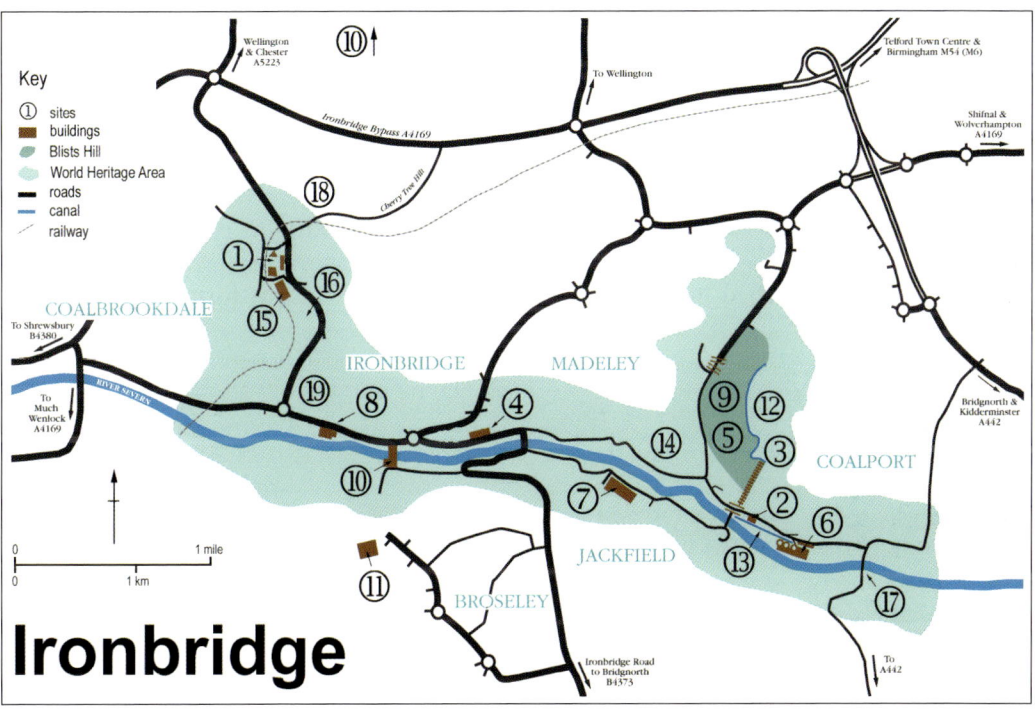

Map of the Ironbridge Gorge showing the location of the digs mentioned in this book. The numbers refer to the dig sections. (Base map © Ironbridge Gorge Museum Trust)

Dig 1

The Old Furnace
(1959–2009)

The Old Furnace is one of the best-known and most iconic industrial archaeology monuments in Britain. Sometimes known as the Darby Furnace or the Upper Furnace, this is where Abraham Darby (1678–1717) perfected in 1709 the use of coke rather than charcoal as a fuel in an iron blast furnace. When combined with his patent of

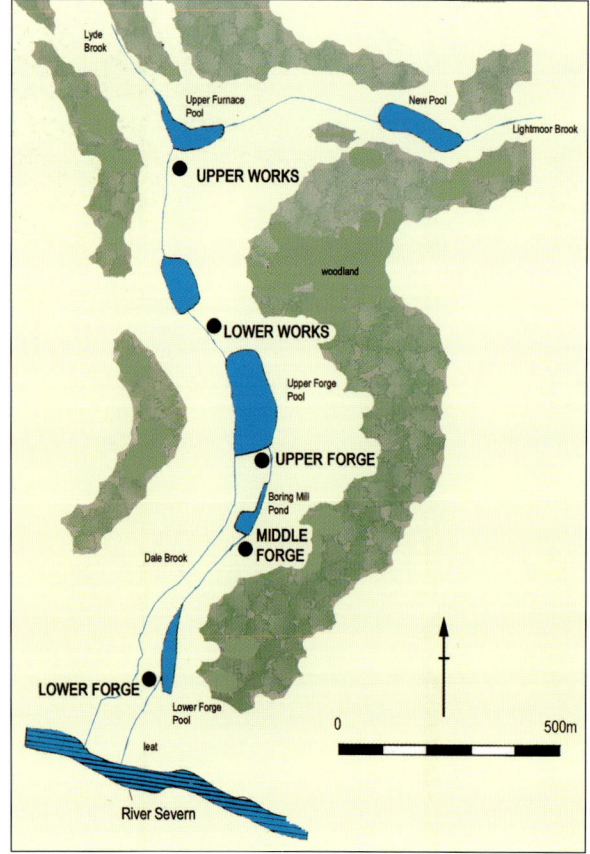

Map of the post-medieval and industrial period forge and furnace sites located along the Dale Brook at Coalbrookdale.

1707 for moulding thin-walled pots using cold greensand, it allowed him to build the first dedicated general iron foundry in Britain. This switch from using an organic fuel – charcoal – to an inorganic fuel, in this case coal (which contains much more energy and is much more abundant), was at the heart of the fuel revolution that helped to spur industrialisation. The Old Furnace, though, is just one of a series of seventeenth- and eighteenth-century forge and furnace sites that lie along the Dale Brook at the western end of the Gorge. Together they form the heart of Ironbridge's reputation for innovation in metal working (Clark, 1993, 42–45; Griffin, 2018, 103–104; Williams, 2017a; see Dig 15, Dig 16, and Dig 19).

The brick- and stone-built square-plan stack of the Old Furnace still stands over 6 metres high, although originally it was several metres taller. It is now protected by a glass and steel pyramid-shaped roof, erected in 1981–82. The surviving elements of

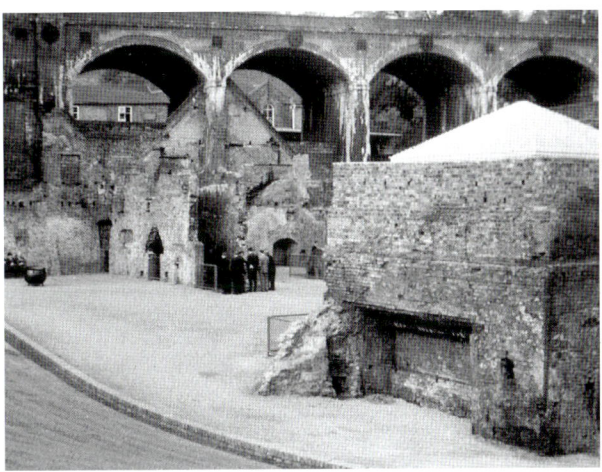

Right: The surviving fabric of the seventeenth- and eighteenth-century Old Furnace in the Upper Forge in 1959 after clearance and restoration. This was the first part of the Gorge to open as a museum. (Image courtesy of Michael S. Darby)

Below: The pyramid covering of the Old Furnace, installed in 1982. The brick wall behind is the revetment for the Upper Furnace Pool dam, whilst the arches of the Wellington & Severn Junction Railway can be seen on the left.

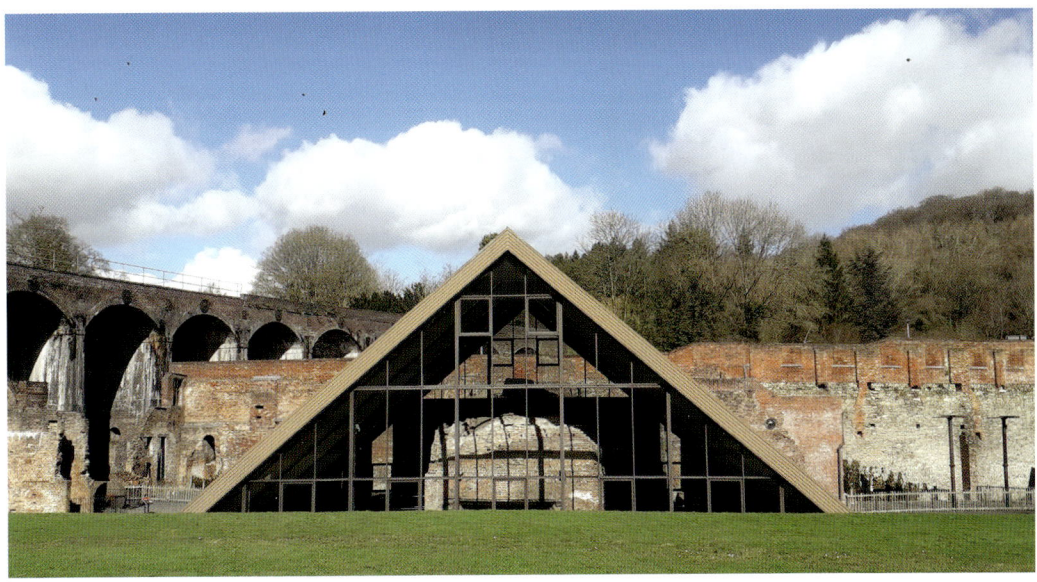

the site include the Old Furnace, the charging platform to the north, and the abutting Upper Furnace Pool dam wall. The furnace structure comprises a double cone, circular in section, built in fire brick surrounded by several courses of hard red brick. The space between the circular cone and the square outer casing, *c.* 9 metres by 9.5 metres in plan, is packed with stone rubble as a fire-resistant material. At ground level there are recesses on three sides of the furnace tower. One, facing east, is for the forehearth, which allowed iron to be bailed out with handheld ladles to make small castings. The other two, which face north and south, are tuyere recesses. A tuyere was the nozzle through which cold air was forced by the bellows into the blast furnace to raise the temperature of the furnace to its working level of 1,500 degrees Celsius. The bellows were powered by a waterwheel, which lay on the western side of the furnace and was fed by a trough or launder from the dam to the north.

The eastern and southern recesses are each spanned by cast-iron beams. One of the four beams above the eastern forehearth recess has the inscription 'BWE 1638 EWB' cast on it. The 1638 date should read 1658 – it was altered sometime in the 1950s during the initial phase of conservation works, when the inscription was repainted in

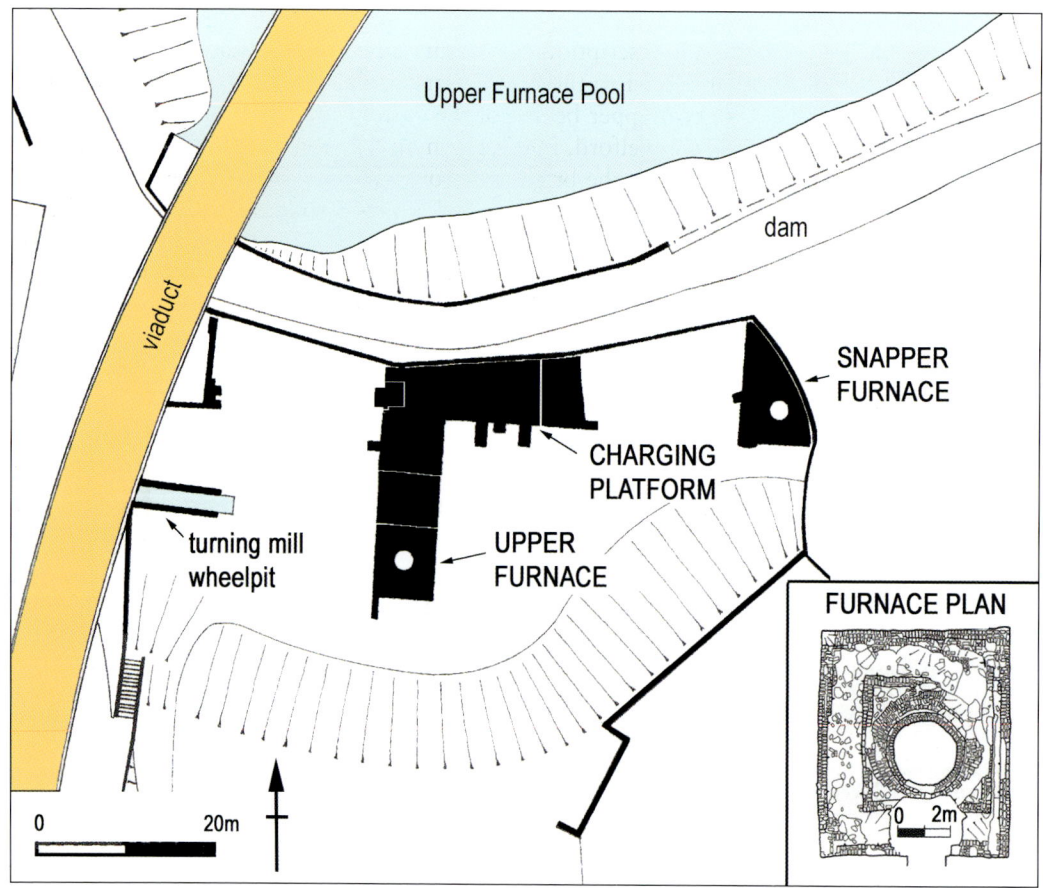

Plan of the Old Furnace complex showing the Upper Furnace and its charging platform, the Snapper Furnace to the east and the Turning Mill foundations to the west.

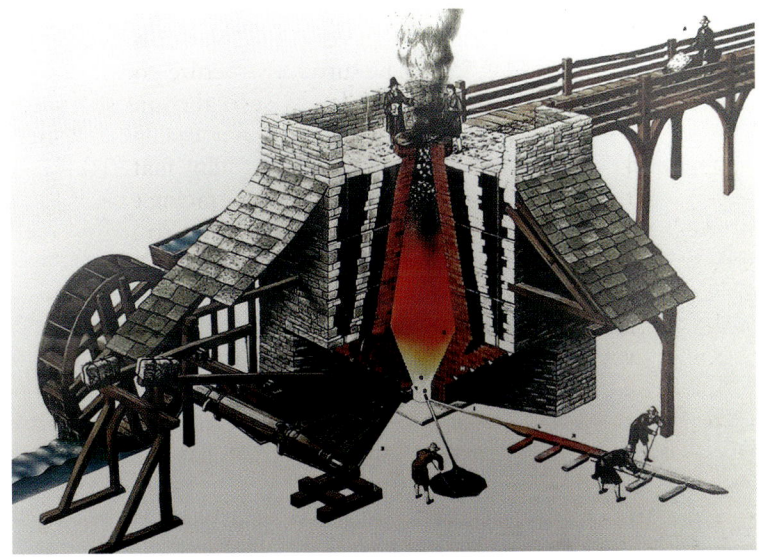

A suggested reconstruction of how the Old Furnace would have functioned in the eighteenth century. (© Ironbridge Gorge Museum Trust)

white. The 'BWE 1638 EWB' inscription also occurs on one of the beams in the southern recess. The letters probably refer to the Brooke family who built the first charcoal blast furnace on this site. The two upper beams of the eastern forehearth are each inscribed 'ABRAHAM DARBY 1777' (Belford, 2007; Hayman, Horton & White, 1999, 22).

To the north of the furnace is the brick and stone charging platform, which survives to over 8 metres high and is 18 metres long and 7.5 metres wide. This was used to bring iron ore, coke, and limestone to fill, or charge, the furnace for firing. On the eastern side of the charging platform is a brick- and stone-built extension, which includes the northern gable end of the moulding and casting rooms added in 1777 by Abraham Darby III (1750–89). The charging platform abuts the pool dam wall and runs east to

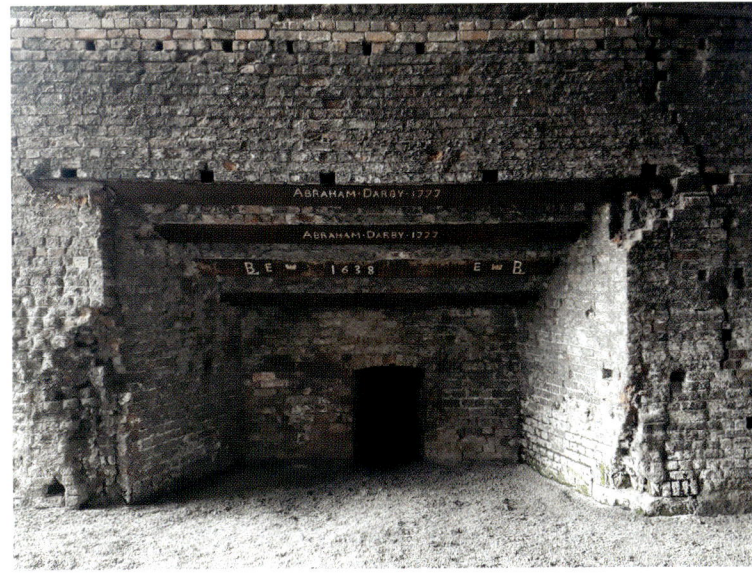

The lintels above the forehearth of the Upper Furnace. The date of '1638' was introduced during the 1950s restoration when the inscriptions were renewed in white paint.

west across the valley with a road running along the top giving access to the charging platform. At the western end of the dam lie the remains of the water-powered turning mill, dating from the 1720s and used for boring the cylinders cast at the furnace. At the eastern end of the dam lies the unfinished snapper furnace dating from 1793, which was intended to supplement the main furnace output in times of high demand (Hayman, Horton & White, 1999, 22–28; Belford, 2007, 137–138).

The modern exploration, conservation, and understanding of the Ironbridge industrial landscape began with the saving of the Old Furnace. This was the first part of the Gorge to be preserved, in 1959, when Allied Ironfounders Ltd, the owners of the site, opened a small museum around the furnace to mark the 250th anniversary of Abraham Darby I's first smelting at the Old Furnace using coke. This early piece of industrial heritage conservation involved removing several meters of spoil from the demolition of the foundry buildings around the furnace that had been dumped here in the 1930s, ironically an act that helped to preserve its structure. In 1959 a new drainage system was installed around the furnace, to help dry the structure, along with steps to the provide access to the top of the furnace. Here a glazed cap covered the cone to protect it from the weather.

In 1970 the whole Coalbrookdale Upper Works, of which the Old Furnace was a central feature, became part of the Ironbridge Gorge Museum Trust, but archaeological recording, as well as further heritage conservation, had to await the 1980s. Limited archaeological work was undertaken in 1981–82 in and around the blast furnace,

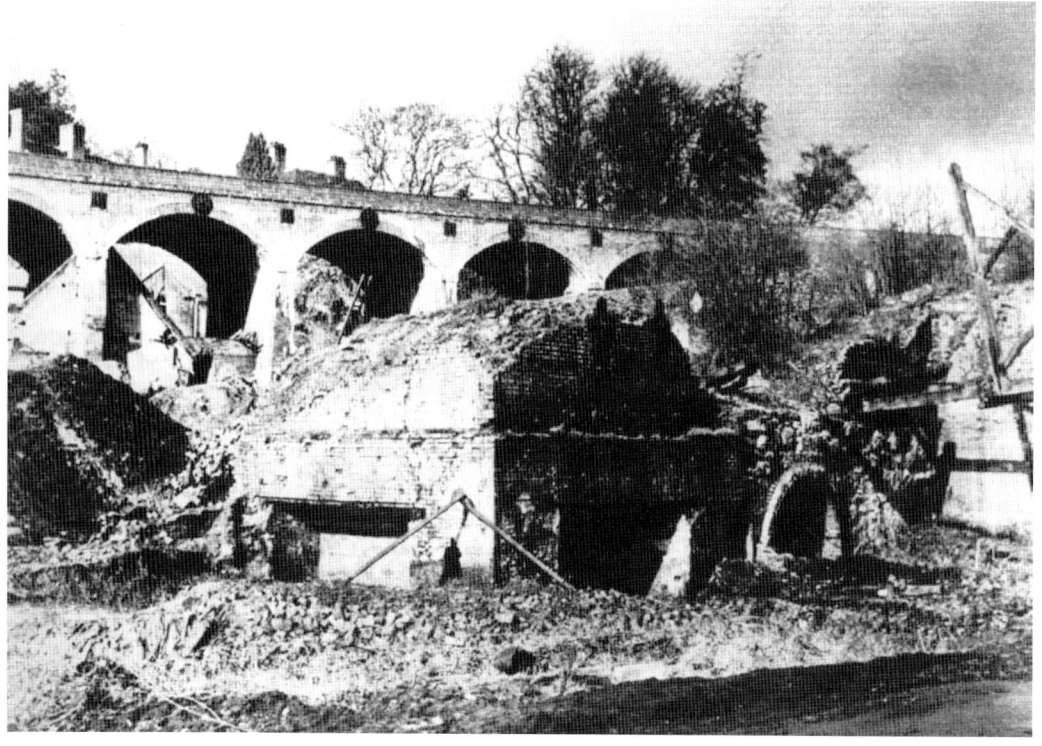

The Old Furnace in 1951 before clearance of over a metre of rubble and restation work began later in the decade. (© Michael S. Darby)

when the narrow foundations for the new steel and glass building that would cover the furnace were being dug. Between 2.5 metres and 3 metres of deposits were noted around the furnace base, with the lowest deposits containing charcoal layers that might be associated with the original 1658 charcoal blast furnace and the associated casting floors. The upper layers were dominated by dumping from slag and black sand used in the adjacent nineteenth-century foundry. A partial collapse of the eastern dam wall in 1987 led to further archaeological recording of this part of the complex. Three small trenches were dug around the charging ramp extension to the east of the Old Furnace. Trench 1, at the eastern end of the ramp extension, was the most interesting, revealing a brick floor beneath which was a layer of sand sealing a brick drain at a depth of 0.5 metres. Pottery suggested that these features dated to the mid-eighteenth to nineteenth centuries. These remains are probably associated with the casting and moulding shops erected in this area during the eighteenth century and then converted in the nineteenth century into storerooms (Hayman, Horton & White, 1999, 11–38; Trueman, Jones & MacLeod, 1988).

Between 1992 and 1994 more extensive archaeological work was undertaken by the Ironbridge Archaeology Unit as part of the Severn Gorge Repairs Project. This work focussed on detailed building and fabric recording of the Old Furnace, charging ramp, snapper furnace, turning mill, and Upper Furnace Pool dam wall (Hayman, Horton & White, 1999, 21–22). It demonstrated that the outer wall of the Old Furnace contained both original fabric from the mid-seventeenth century and from the 1708–09 Darby

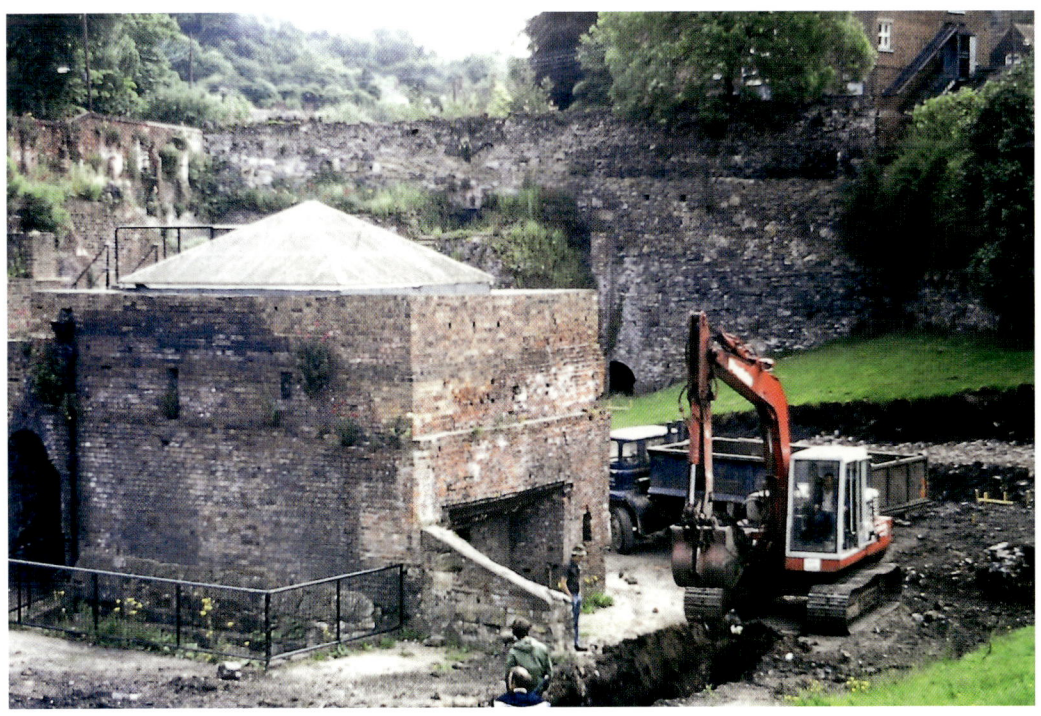

Archaeological work in 1982 ahead of the building of the current pyramidal roof over the Old Furnace. (© Ironbridge Gorge Museum Trust)

rebuild. However, much of the fabric of the furnace cone dates to a rebuild from 1777, with further repairs from 1810. Investigation of the drainage trenches excavated between the charging platform and the snapper furnace threw further light on the remains found in 1987. These revealed the walls of foundry buildings abutting the charging platform and a cast-iron flask from the foundry (Hayman, Horton & White, 1999, 31–33).

In 2008 and 2009 limited archaeological excavations were undertaken prior to improvements in the access to and interpretation of the site. This work involved new walkways, new ground surfaces, and changes to the covering furnace building. Thirteen trenches were excavated, five around the Old Furnace itself, two to the east, two to the south, and four to the west of this structure. No evidence for any pre-1709 activity was found, but a culvert and wall were located just outside the south-eastern corner of the Old Furnace in Trench 4. These two features may have been part of the later stages of the furnace's working life after 1777 but were more likely inserted after the furnace went out of use in 1818. Exterior and interior features were also found for the post-furnace workshop buildings in Trenches 5, 6, 7, and 10 (Belford, 2009a).

Research in the 2010s by Richard Williams on the process residues excavated from the Old Furnace site has shown that Abraham Darby I's rebuilt 1709 furnace almost certainly ran at much the same hearth temperature as contemporary charcoal furnaces but produced iron with a higher-silicon content than that from charcoal iron furnaces. This difference was critical for the casting of thin pots in sand (Williams, 2017a, 22–23). However, Darby's foundry-orientated method of working, rather than just focussing on cast-iron pig production, meant that he frequently had to keep his furnace hot while the Upper Furnace pool filled up, reducing production, meaning that the furnace produced much less than the 8–9 tonnes a week the size of the furnace size might suggest (Williams, 2017b, 87–88). Nevertheless, the combination of a coke-fired blast furnace attached to a foundry with air furnaces laid the foundations for the future mass production of cast iron, which his son and grandson exploited.

The Old Furnace is regarded as the most significant eighteenth-century iron furnace in Britain because of its pioneering role in the use of coke for iron smelting. The archaeological research and recording since 1959 complements the documentary evidence to show that the Old Furnace was regularly repaired and improved between 1658 and 1818. After the 1709 rebuild the best known of these adaptations was in 1777, when Abraham Darby III rebuilt it to a new design in preparation for making castings for the Iron Bridge. The legacy of production at the Upper Works furnace remains impressive. It was the first complex to bore cylinders for stationary steam engines, the first to manufacture iron wheels for wagons, and the first to cast iron rails. Yet, the Darby family's pioneering work was part of a much longer tradition of innovation in the valley, dating back to Brooke's seventeenth-century steelworks, and further to the very first charcoal-fired iron furnaces in the area built during the sixteenth century (Belford, 2018).

Dig 2

Tar Tunnel Excavation (1965–74)

The Tar Tunnel at Coalport is probably the most unusual heritage feature in the Gorge. Entered through a doorway in the cellar of a shop, on the northern side of the Coalport Canal (Dig 13), the tunnel gives access to a spring of natural bitumen. This is a substance made from the remains of microscopic plants and animals buried by sediment in marine basins and freshwater lakes millions of years ago. Once common in the Gorge, and elsewhere in western Shropshire, this is now the only accessible surviving source. It was discovered in 1786 by workman digging a horizontal tunnel at river level from a meadow in Madeley. It was designed to link up with the vertical shafts sunk by ironmaster William Reynolds, grandson of Abraham Darby II, to access coal seams beneath Blists Hill, one of several mines sunk in the area by the ironmaster during the late eighteenth century (see Dig 9). The intention was to meet these shafts at a depth of *c.* 45 metres and thereby reduce the cost of hauling the coal up from the deep mine. It was intended that the tunnel would form an underground canal, like the ones at Worsley

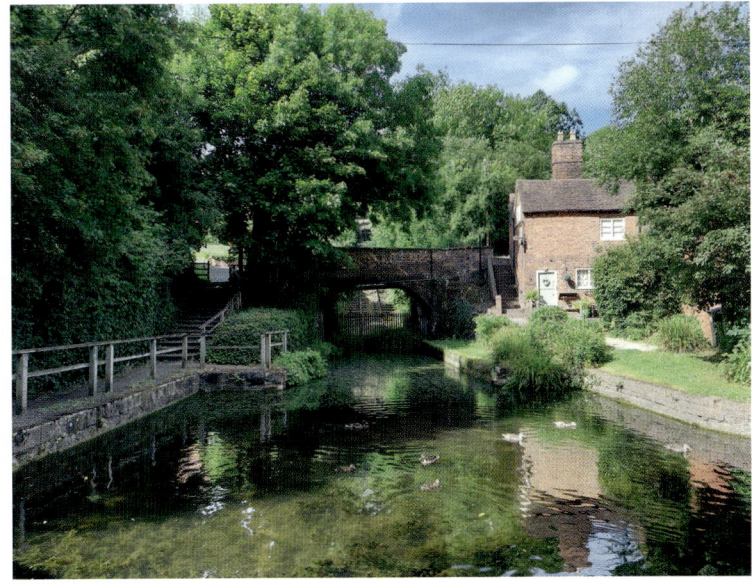

The western end of the Coalport Canal (Dig 13) where it meets the bottom of the Hay Inclined Plane (Dig 3) under the road bridge. Access to the Tar Tunnel, dug in the 1790s, is through the brick buildings to the right of the bridge.

on the Bridgewater Canal, and that the coal would be taken out on boats onto the River Severn. However, after digging for roughly 275 metres, the workman hit a natural bitumen spring (Hadfield, 1966, 152–153; Trinder, 2000, 105–106).

The bitumen spring quickly became a scientific sensation, being declared by Samuel More, Secretary of the Society of Arts, in a letter to Abraham Darby III, to be far superior to tar made from coal. Visited by many other scientists in the next few years it became a Georgian tourist hotspot and one of the wonders of the Gorge. Producing as much as 4,500 gallons (*c.* 20,450 litres) a week in the 1790s, Reynolds processed the tar, collecting it in wells and once outside the tunnel, boiling it in large cauldrons to convert it into pitch. It was then sold as 'Native Tar' for use in preserving timber or processed to make a substance like lamp black for use in lamps, or as a varnish. It was even used in medicinal preparations for the treatment of rheumatic and skin conditions. The Madeley Wood Company bought the 'Native Tar Concern' in 1805 and although production declined, tar was still being extracted in small quantities as late as 1843. This product was, though, just a secondary feature of the tunnel, its main use being as a railway, not a canal, for taking coal out of the mines and as a drainage channel from the mine. Such early railways are sometimes called plateways, tramways, or wagonways, although none of these terms appear in use in the Gorge before the mid-nineteenth century. These early rails were wooden or a wood and iron composite, although from the 1760s the Coalbrookdale Company manufactured all-iron rails (Dig 10). The wagons were pulled by horses or sometimes pushed by hand along the track. The Tar Tunnel and its railway remained in use until the Blists Hill Mine closed in 1941 and was reused briefly in the early 1940s as an air-raid shelter.

The Tar Tunnel was first explored by the Shropshire Mining Club in 1965, members venturing over 640 metres past rock and clay falls and stalactites. Dawley District Council, precursor of Telford Development Corporation, purchase the tunnel and the cottage at its entrance in 1967 and the first 90 metres were cleared and made available for tours led by IGMT in 1969. In 1974 the National Coal Board further cleared the tunnel up to 275 metres into the hillside. During this work rails were laid to remove the rubble and these can still be seen in the twenty-first century.

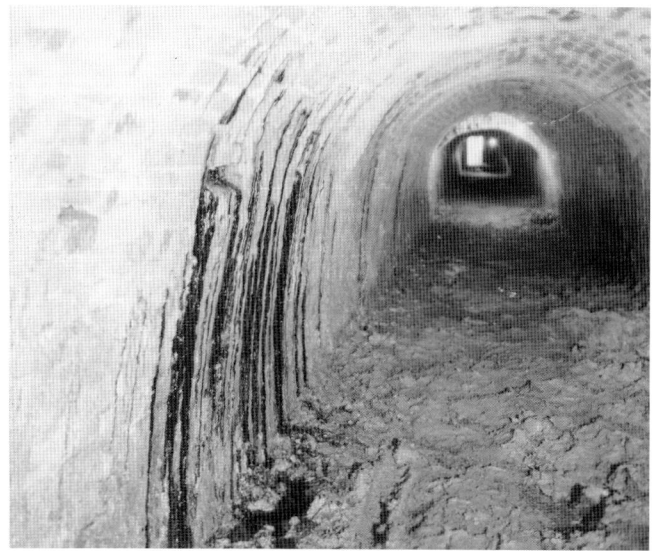

The interior of the Tar Tunnel looking south towards the entrance in 1974, taken by Brian Bracegirdle. Note the tar seeping through the brickwork on the left-hand side of the tunnel. (© and courtesy of Pat Bracegirdle)

The tunnel, which ran for around 1 kilometre, was brick-lined for the first *c.* 300 metres, with a double skin of bricks at the entrance running for just 18 metres. This was perhaps to strengthen the tunnel as it passed underneath a road. Here, the brick tunnel is 1.8 metres (6 feet) high and arched with a water channel to one side. At around 246 metres, the tunnel widens to more than 3.6 metres (12 feet), to allow a double track for wagons to pass each other. Beyond this section the tunnel narrows again and is unlined for 420 metres before more brick lining is encountered. Thereafter, the tunnel is no more than a brick-lined drainage channel 0.9 metres (3 feet) across. A side passage, blocked by a roof fall, runs off the main tunnel 361 metres in, and almost certainly gave access to the Blists Hill lower coal shaft. Visitors in the twenty-first century can no longer access the tunnel, but peering down it from the entrance it is possible to still see the tar seeping through the mortar joints between the brick tunnel lining.

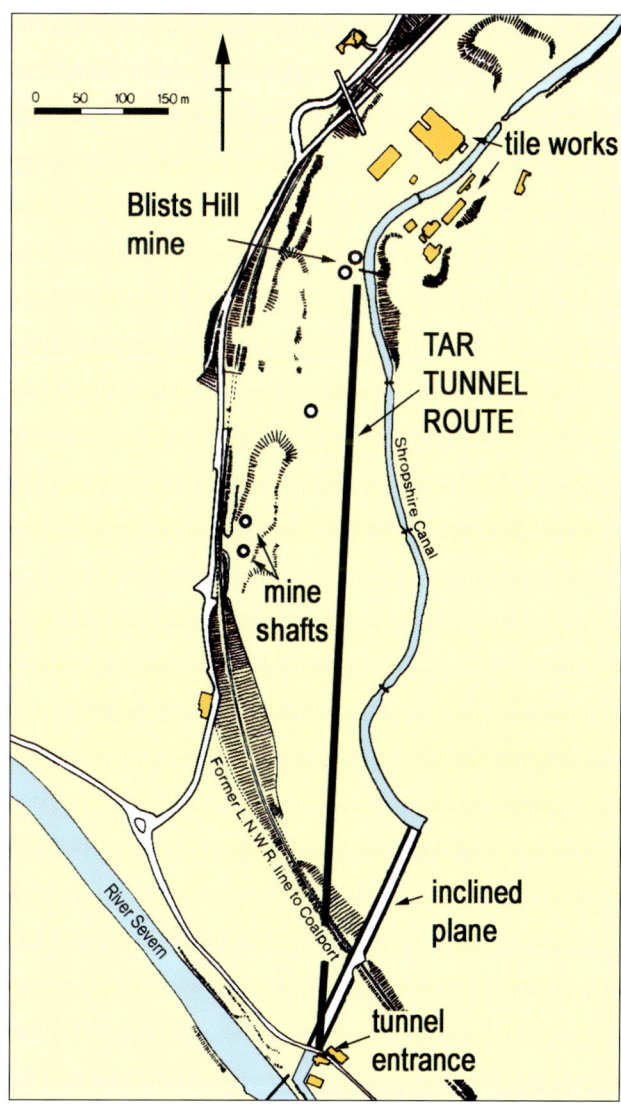

Map of the 1790s Tar Tunnel route from its entrance at Coalport to Blists Hill Mines.

Dig 3

Hay Inclined Plane and Blists Hill Canal (1968–95)

The Hay Inclined Plane is one of the most spectacular industrial sites in the Gorge, the double-track tram or railway rising 82 metres over 320 metres up the steep valley side from the River Severn to a canal basin at the Hay. It forms part of the Shropshire Canal and was built in 1790–91 as one of three such inclined planes along the route of the canal (Hadfield, 1966, 153–154; Trinder 2000, 70).

The 17.7 km length of the Shropshire Canal crossed uneven and hilly terrain and the use of inclined planes was preferred to building a more expensive series of locks (Hadfield, 1966, 152–159). In part promoted by the Coalbrookdale Iron Company, it seems likely that the existence of extensive colliery railways along the Gorge by the late eighteenth century, many of them built by the company, made the use of inclines to carry barges seem feasible. The Hay Inclined Plane was the steepest and longest-lived of the Shropshire Canal planes, and enabled canal traffic from Blists Hill to link with the river transport on the Severn at the Coalport China Works (see Dig 6). The track was repaired and re-laid several times, including after the London & North Western Railway took

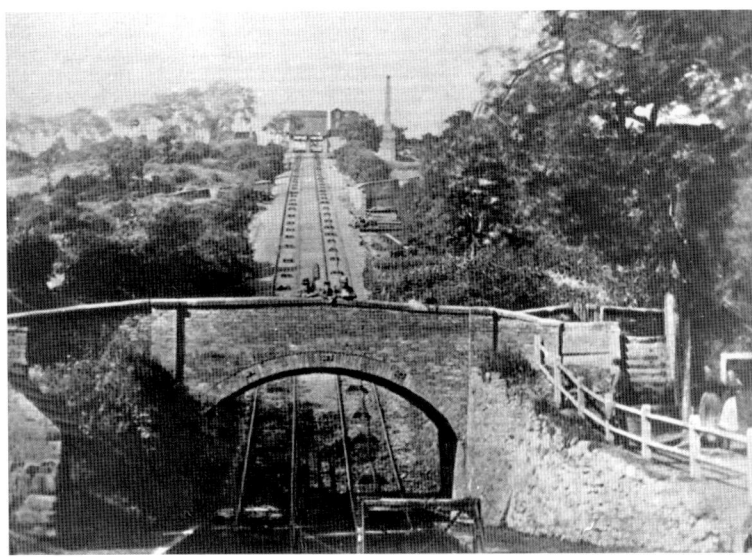

The Hay Inclined plane in the 1870s looking northwards from the Coalport Canal. The winding engine house and chimney can be seen at the top of the incline. (© Ironbridge Gorge Museum Trust)

over the canal in 1857. It fell into disuse in 1894 and was officially closed in 1907, most of the rails being removed in 1910 and the engine house and boilers were demolished by the 1950s (Hadfield, 1966, 238; Hayman, Horton & White, 1999, 125–135).

The incline comprises three major elements. At the northern, top end lies a canal basin, an engine house, boiler settings and chimney stack, a northern building, and two loading bays. All these features were brick-built. A double track then runs for approximately 320 metres down the valley side. At the foot of this trackway lies a second, lower canal basin. The only stretches of track that date to its operation as part of the canal are at the very top and at the bottom of the incline.

Restoration work on the Hay Inclined Plane began in 1968 and the central section of track bed was laid by the Territorial Army in 1969, which involved bringing in 3,000 tons of material to rebuild it, although no archaeological recording was undertaken. Tracks were re-laid by volunteers in 1975 and the initial conservation also included work on the stone-built upper basin canal walls and clearing the lower canal basin. This work was completed in 1976. Detailed archaeological recording, however, did not take place until the 1990s. Excavation work at the top end of the incline was undertaken in 1995, recording the loading bays, brick-built engine bed, and the site of the boilers.

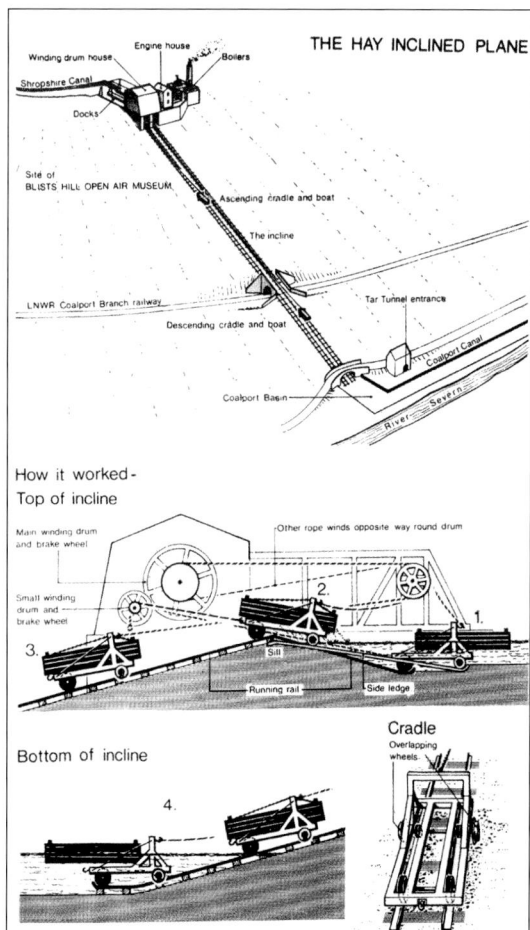

A suggested reconstruction of how the Inclined Plane worked when built in the 1790s. (© Ironbridge Gorge Museum Trust)

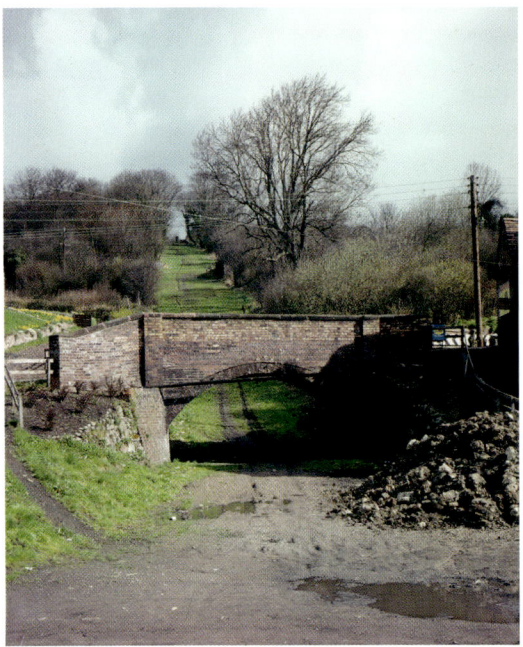 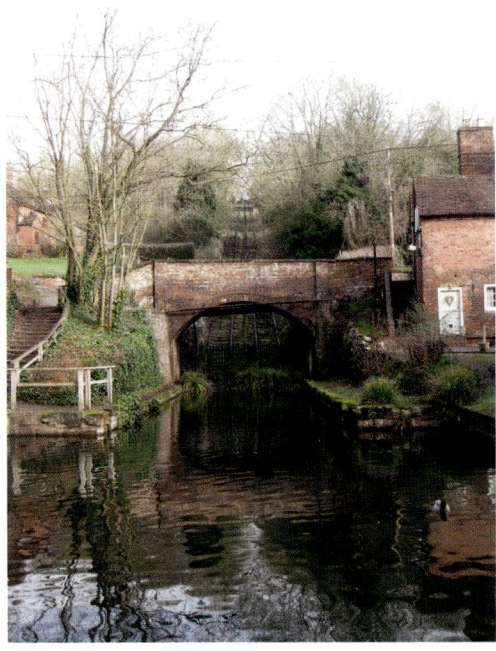

Above left: The bottom of the Hay Inclined Plane where it meets the western end of the Coalport Canal in 1974 before restoration. Taken by Brian Bracegirdle. (© Pat Bracegirdle)

Above right: The same view in 2020 of the bottom of the Hay Inclined Plane where it meets the western end of the Coalport Canal after restoration.

This allowed the development of the power system of the incline to be traced, from the initial horse-driven phase of 1791–92, to the installation of the stationary steam engine in 1792–93 built to a design by Adam Heslop (see Dig 9) using a flywheel to haul the boat, which involved altering parts of the upper basin and the loading bays. The upper complex was remodelled in the period 1835–47 when two new boilers, a square chimney stack and a new engine house were built on the eastern side of the basin (Clark, 1993, 100–101).

One of the many geological faults that run across the Gorge can be found passing through the top basin of the inclined plane, causing problems with collapsing walls. This probably explains the leakages noted in the canal in the 1980s and early 1990s. Three stop locks were excavated when the line of the canal north of the incline was repaired in 1992. These are locations where timber planks could be swung by crane or by hand to block off sections for maintenance or to stop water draining away if there was a breach. The southern and northern stop locks each had centrally placed vertical iron slots to talk the stop plans (Horton et al, 1993). The locks each formed a narrowing of the canal to make the job of putting in the stop lock easier. Both were built from random coursed limestone blocks, some of which had mason's marks.

The restoration of the line of the canal allowed the basin at Blists Hill to be filled with water and gave access to the towpath towards the Hay Inclined Plane, from where spectacular views of the eastern end of the Gorge are visible during the winter. Today this stretch of canal is partially filled with water and is dominated by reeds, a reminder of how quickly such industrial transport networks can return to nature.

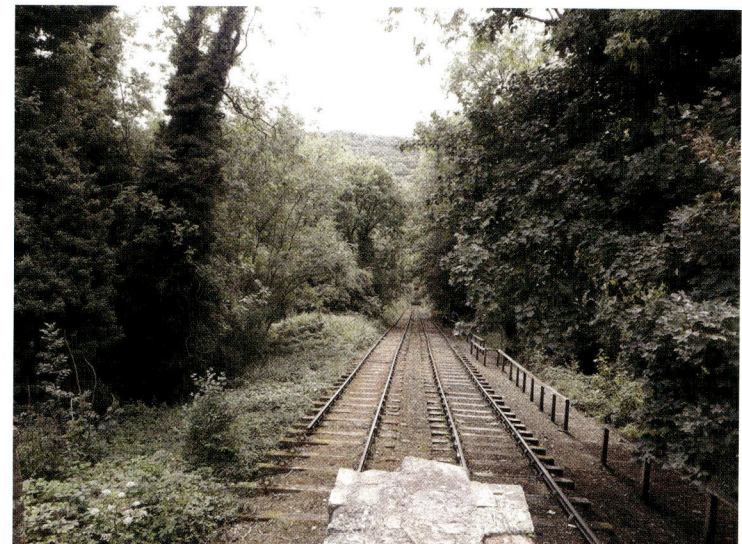

The Hay Inclined Plane in 2020 looking down the valley towards the Coalport Canal, showing the twin tracks after restoration.

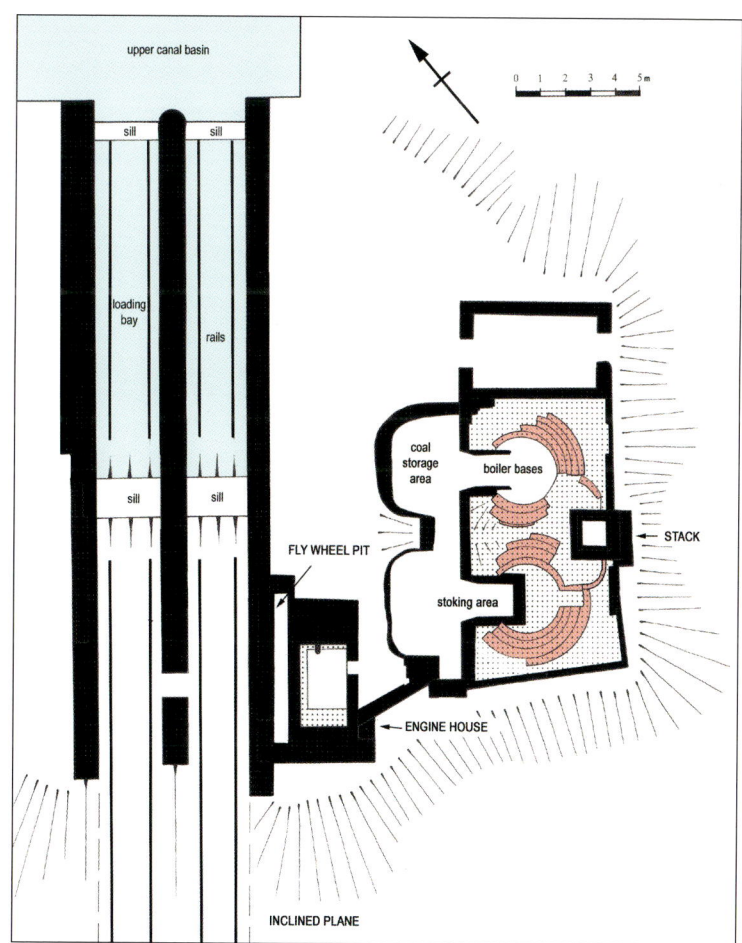

Excavation plan of the Hay Inclined Plane winding engine house. Note the two haystack boiler bases, square chimney base, and the engine house.

Dig 4

Bedlam Furnaces (1971–2015)

Terraced into the steep northern bank of the River Severn, roughly 700 metres east of the Iron Bridge and surrounded by woodland, lie the ruins of one of the most evocative iron-making sites within the Gorge: the Bedlam Furnaces, the local name for the Madeley Wood Ironworks. These form the second oldest visible set of furnaces within the Gorge, after the Darby furnaces. The ironworks was founded as the Madeley

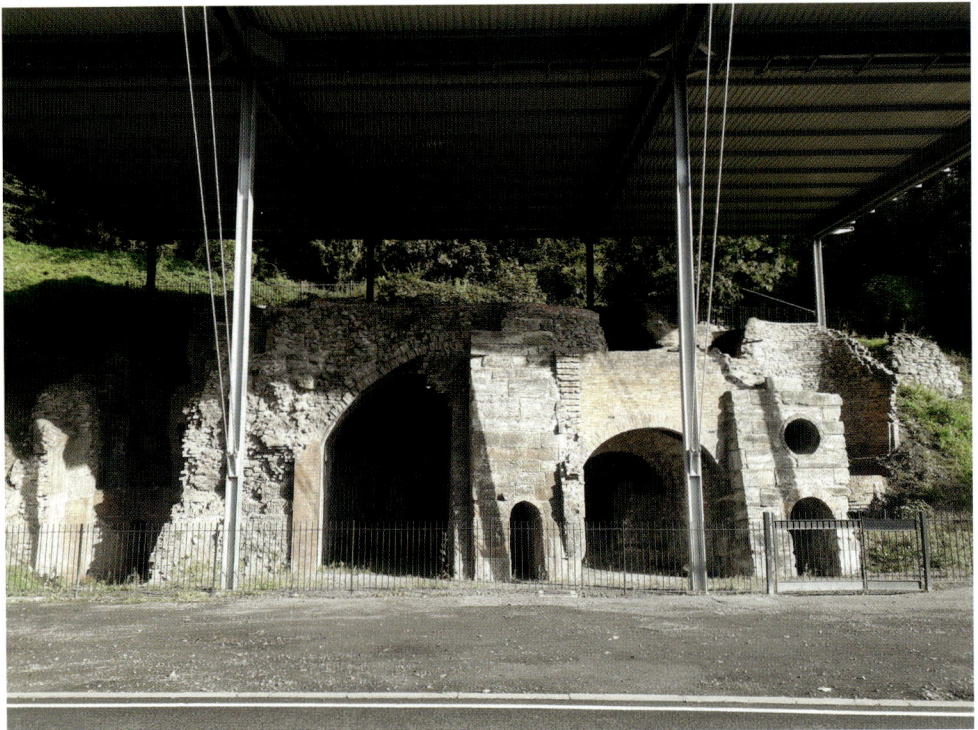

The southern, front elevation of the eighteenth-century Bedlam Furnaces under its early twenty-first-century roof. The engine house lies on the left with the blowing house arch in the middle and the Furnace I arch on the right of the picture.

Wood Furnace Company in 1757, taken over by the Dale Company in 1776, and then run by William Reynolds & Co. after 1794. This was a firm with extensive industrial interests in the Gorge including coal mining at Blists Hill to the east. In its final form the ironworks was run by the Madeley Wood Company from 1803 until its closure in 1843, when only a single furnace was in operation. The demolition of part of the site followed soon after closure, with the casting houses and smithy having disappeared by 1847 (Hayman, Horton & White 1999, 58–59).

The ruins visible at Bedlam in the early twenty-first century lie on two levels. The upper level gave access to the top of the furnaces to allow charging with fuel, whilst the lower level gave access to the base of the furnaces and the casting floors. These remains comprise two tower furnaces, separated by an open tuyere chamber, a wheel pit for a waterwheel to run the two sets of bellows, a northern pair of bridgehouses accessed by a railway, and to the south a single casting room and moulding room. A smithy and a steam engine house lay to the west and further railways gave access to the southern river frontage also from the west.

The site has attracted the interest of artists since the beginning of the nineteenth century when it was still working and drew the attention of historians in the later nineteenth century after the works had been abandoned (Trinder, 2017). It is amongst the earliest sites in the Gorge to receive archaeological and conservation attention. From 1971 to 1979 major repairs and limited archaeological work were undertaken. This involved clearing several metres of spoil and debris from the front, southern, elevation of the site, and recording the two furnaces. There was also extensive rebuilding of many

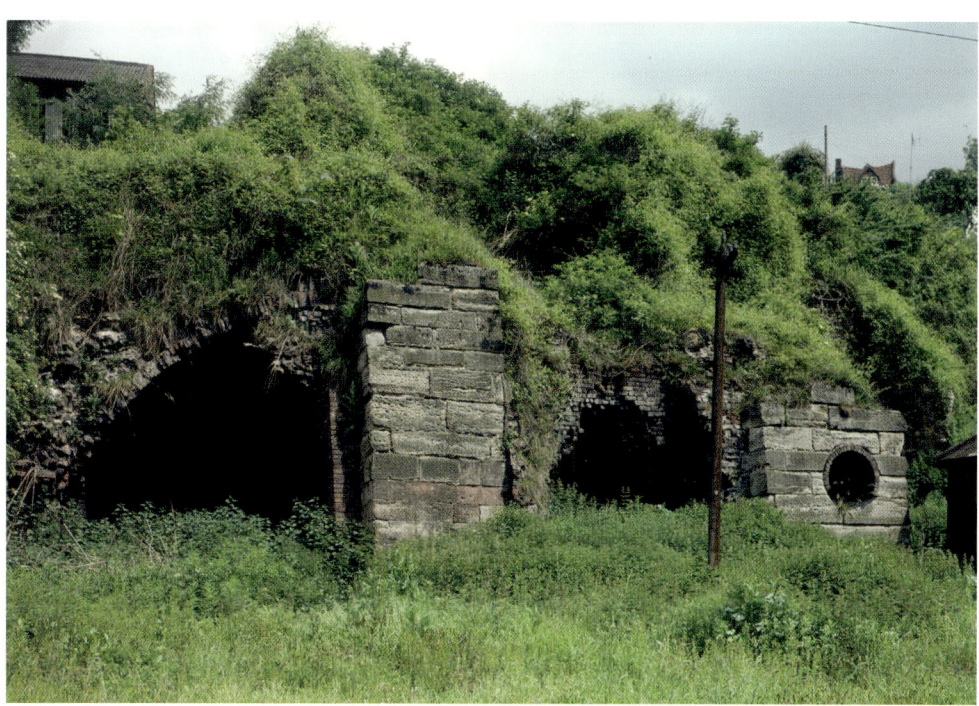

The southern elevation of the Bedlam Furnaces in 1969 before restoration, showing the engine house, blowing house, and furnace buried by more than a metre of rubble. Taken by Brian Bracegirdle. (© Pat Bracegirdle)

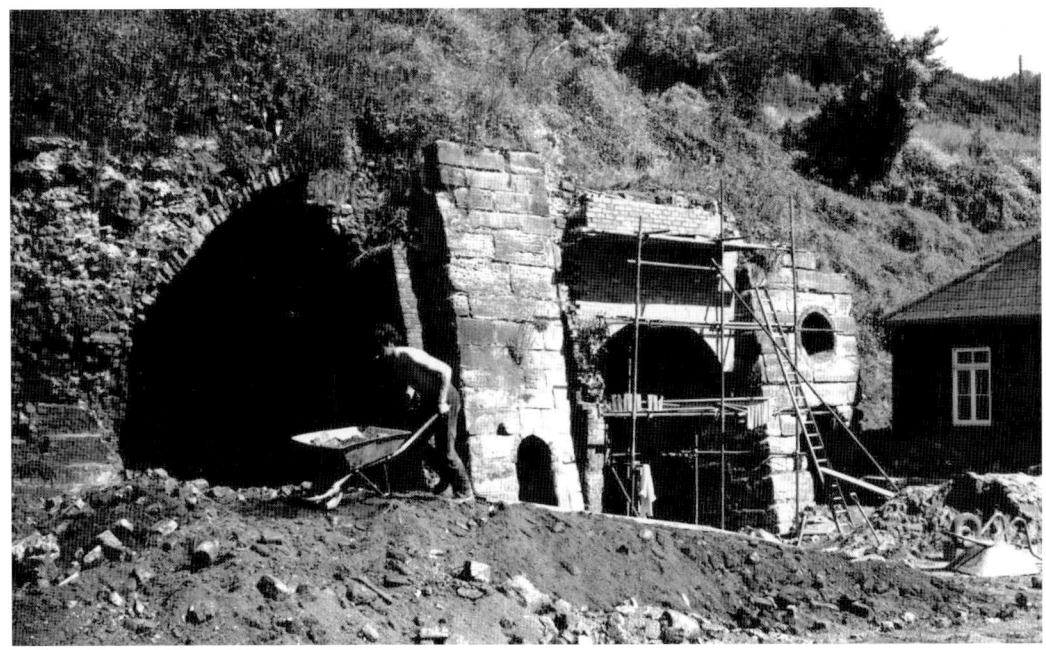

Bedlam Furnace in 1972 showing the initial excavation and conservation work at Furnace I. Taken by Brian Bracegirdle. (© Pat Bracegirdle)

of the upper sections of the exposed stonework. In 1985 the charging houses were cleared and recorded, whilst in 1986 a section of wooden railway was uncovered west of the furnaces during the installation of a gas main. It comprised oak sleepers and wooden rails and was dated to around 1760, when the furnaces were first built (Jones, 1987).

The most extensive archaeological recording was undertaken during the 1990s. From 1993 to 1997 an extensive archaeological survey and excavation of all the key elements of the furnaces was followed by further conservation work (Hayman Horton & White, 1999, 67–82). This explored and consolidated the largely stone-built remains of the steam engine house and engine pit that lie at the western end of the complex. These elements of the site dated from the first phase of work in the late 1750s. The wheel chamber and bellows room lie immediately east of the engine house and belong to this first phase of activity. Documentary and map evidence indicates that the bellows were replaced by a blowing cylinder and water-regulator on this part of the site, although still powered by a waterwheel. However, the archaeological work of the 1990s failed to find evidence for these changes. Beyond the bellows room further to the east is the western Furnace 1 tuyere chamber and Furnace 2. Both furnaces were rebuilt in the late 1810s, the present Furnace 1 lying slightly to the west and overlapping the original western furnace. The tuyere chamber and Furnace 2 were also rebuilt. Furnace 2 retains its tall brick stack, which has a bottle-shaped profile. This is the only surviving example of this type of nineteenth-century blast furnace design, which was also used at other furnace sites in the Gorge. These alterations meant that the engine had to be enlarged or perhaps replaced and is reflected in changes to the design of the engine house (Hayman & Horton, 1999, 33–34).

The site of the coke ovens, and the lost third furnace added in the period 1806–10, lie at the eastern end of the site but have yet to be explored. Above these features on the upper terrace of the site lies the charging platform. The original charging houses were infilled, and the charging platform raised to access the later, taller furnaces. This is the present form of this part of the furnace site.

During the early twenty-first century worries grew about the deterioration of the exposed monument. This led to a scheme to build a roof over the site, which involved further small-scale excavation and fabric recording ahead of the erection of the roof supports. The completion of the scheme in 2015 has produced a monument whose display, beneath a tall roof but open to the elements, is as striking as the 1982 pyramid that protects the original Darby furnace (Dig 1).

It is significant that recent research has shown that the major castings for the Iron Bridge (Dig 20) were made here, when in early September 1778 the first half rib was cast in front of a large crowd (*Shrewsbury Chronicle*, September 1778, de Haan, 2022, in progress). It is likely that the 5.75-ton rib was cast from an air furnace rather than directly from one of the blast furnaces, though all ten half ribs were cast by late October, as recorded by a bill for ale in Abraham Darby's account book (de Hann, 2022).

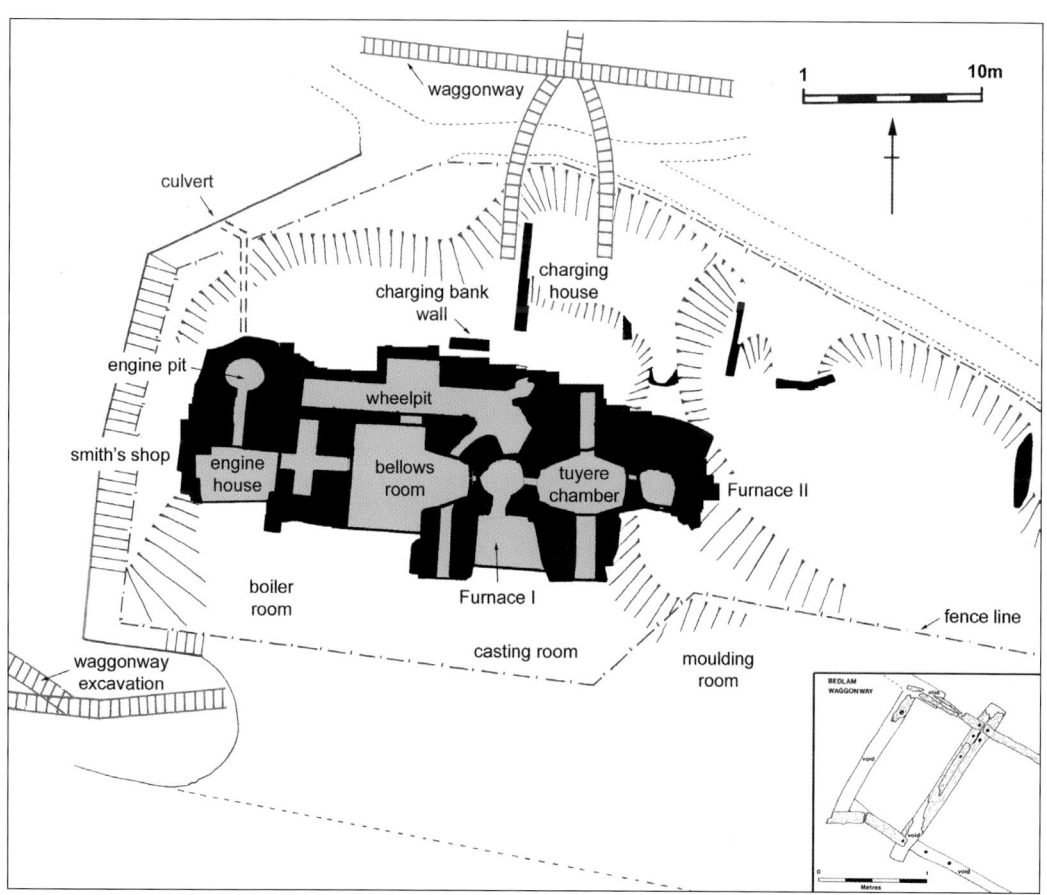

Excavation plan of the Bedlam Furnaces showing the location of the wagonway. Large parts of the Scheduled Ancient Monument remain unexplored.

Dig 5

Blists Hill Blast Furnaces (1973–95)

Blists Hill was the first part of the Ironbridge Gorge Museum Trust to be opened and the site reflects the transport, mining, and manufacturing history of this part of the valley. The line of the abandoned Shropshire Canal, a brick and tile works, the site of the Blists Hill Mine, and the ruinous Blists Hill furnaces were all chosen in 1968 as the location for the open-air museum that would become the heart of the new Ironbridge Gorge Museum Trust. The site was purchased by Telford Development Corporation and the Blists Hill Open Air Museum opened in 1973, when the first excavations at the Blists Hill furnaces site took place. Since then, conserved historic buildings, new buildings, and exhibits have been added to the site, building a living historical picture of a small 1890s and 1900s industrial community (Hayman & Horton, 1999, 59–61, 85–86, 126; Hayman, Horton & White, 1999, 104–106).

Of particular importance was the deep mining of coal, begun at Blists Hill in the 1780s, with ironstone mining starting shortly afterwards. Both these raw materials supplied the neighbouring blast furnaces at Bedlam (Dig 4) and at Blists Hill (Dig 9). In the twenty-first century the standing remains form a striking backdrop to the lower part of the Blists Hill industrial village, terraced into the valley side. At the heart of the ruins are the three square bases on which the iron blast furnaces sat. To the east of these are two charging houses (north and south), and behind these was a calcining kiln. At the northern and southern ends of the complex lie two engine and boiler houses.

The remains of the Blists Hill iron furnaces form the largest, and technologically the latest, of the three visible blast furnace complexes within the Gorge (see Dig 1 and Dig 4). The Madeley Wood Company, which took over the Bedlam Furnace site in 1803, built the technologically more advanced Blists Hill blast furnaces between 1832 and 1844. They chose this site because it was close to the Shropshire Canal and was near to the coal and iron ore mine at Blists Hill. Initially run as an additional site to that at Bedlam, it became the company's main ironworks when the Bedlam furnaces closed in 1843 (Hayman & Horton, 1999, 127–128).

In 1971 the Ironbridge Gorge Museum Trust began clearing and restoring the ironworks in order to incorporate the furnaces into the museum. The first excavation at the furnaces took place in 1973 and involved removing roughly 3.5 metres of demolition overburden to reveal the three furnace bases. This allowed repairs to be undertaken in 1978. The three blast furnace bases were square in plan, roughly 11 metres long on each

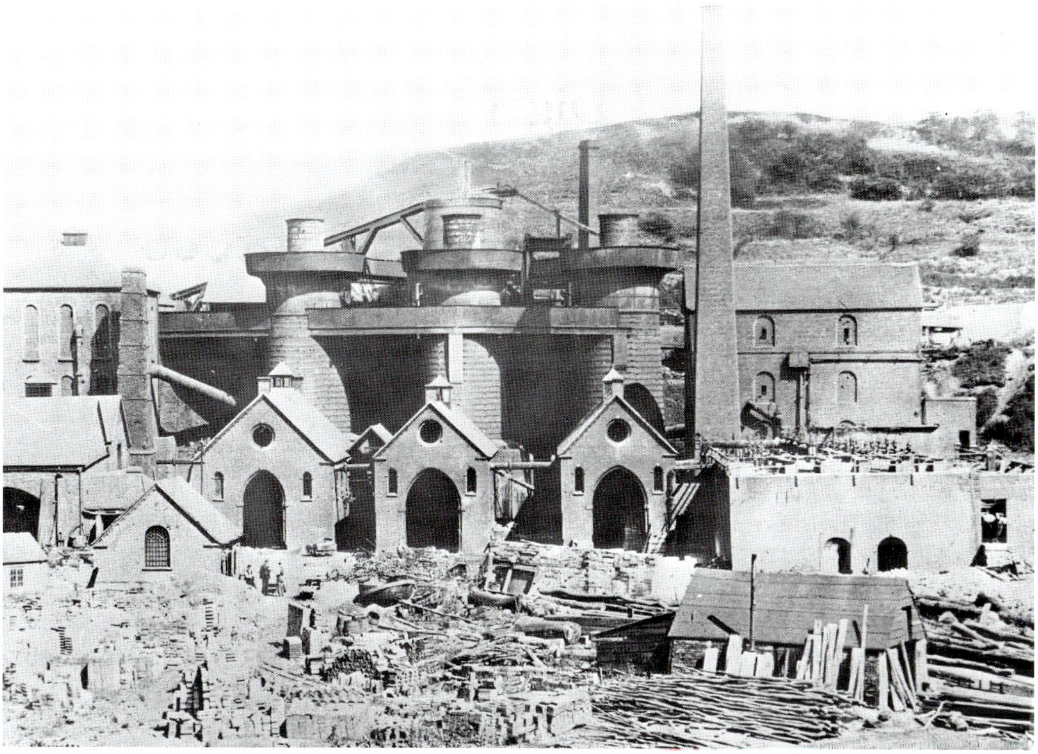

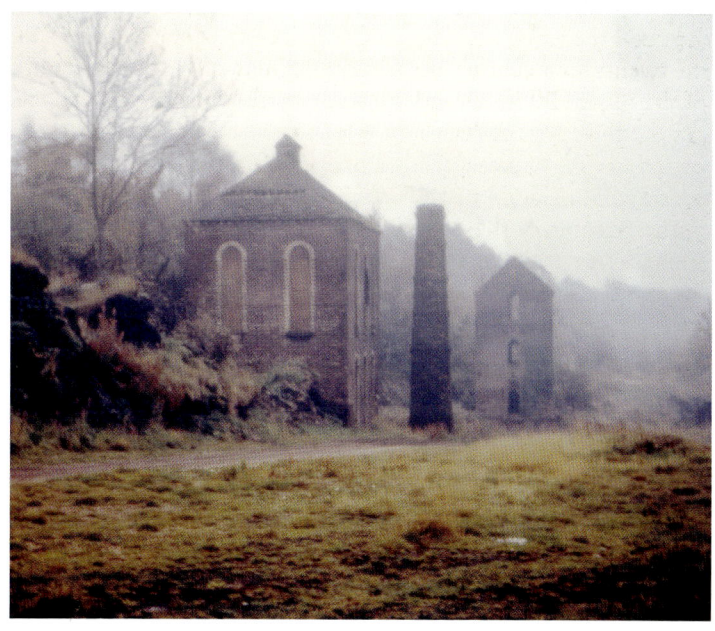

The Blists Hill blast furnaces in the late nineteenth or early twentieth centuries, showing the western elevation. The southern engine house is to the right and the northern engine house to the left. This image shows the rebuilt blast furnaces. (© Ironbridge Gorge Museum Trust)

The Blists Hill blast furnaces in 1964 as captured by Kate Bishop before the founding of the Ironbridge Gorge Museum Trust and before any conservation work. This view shows the northern engine house on the left and its chimney, with the southern engine house in the distance on the right. (© Ironbridge Gorge Museum Trust)

side, with battered walls of hammer-dressed sandstone and arranged in a row, running north to south. There were splayed openings in each face. Those on the western side were for the forehearths. On the remaining sides were openings for the tuyeres, a nozzle through which air was forced into the furnace. A network of brick tunnels beneath the furnace bases prevented ground water from entering the hearths. During the years 1978–80 the three-storey south engine house was restored and re-roofed. This was a brick-built structure, roughly 15 metres by 6.5 metres in plan, with a datestone bearing the inscription '1840' above the southern doorway.

However, a full archaeological survey of the ironworks complex was not undertaken until 1991–95, when all these structures were recorded in detail. The three-storey north engine house, 8 metres by 11 metres in plan, was shown to be a complete rebuild from 1873 on the same footprint as the original engine house from 1833. It retained its detached brick chimney stack by the south-western corner of the building, although the adjacent boiler house was added in the late twentieth century. A vertical steam engine was located in the building in 1971, and rests on a concrete floor obscuring much of the original 1870s engine foundations. However, the interior of the south engine house is largely intact and may echo the layout of the north engine house. This southern building contained a central bob wall on which the cast-iron beam for the engine pivoted. To the north was an engine bed and condenser pit, still containing a fragment of condenser feed pipe. To the south of the bob wall were two blast outlets indicating where the two blowing cylinders were. There was also a rectangular engine bed and condenser pit with, to the west, a flywheel pit. The water for the boilers in each engine house was supplied from the canal above and to the east. This is why the Madeley Wood Company insisted that the Shropshire Canal

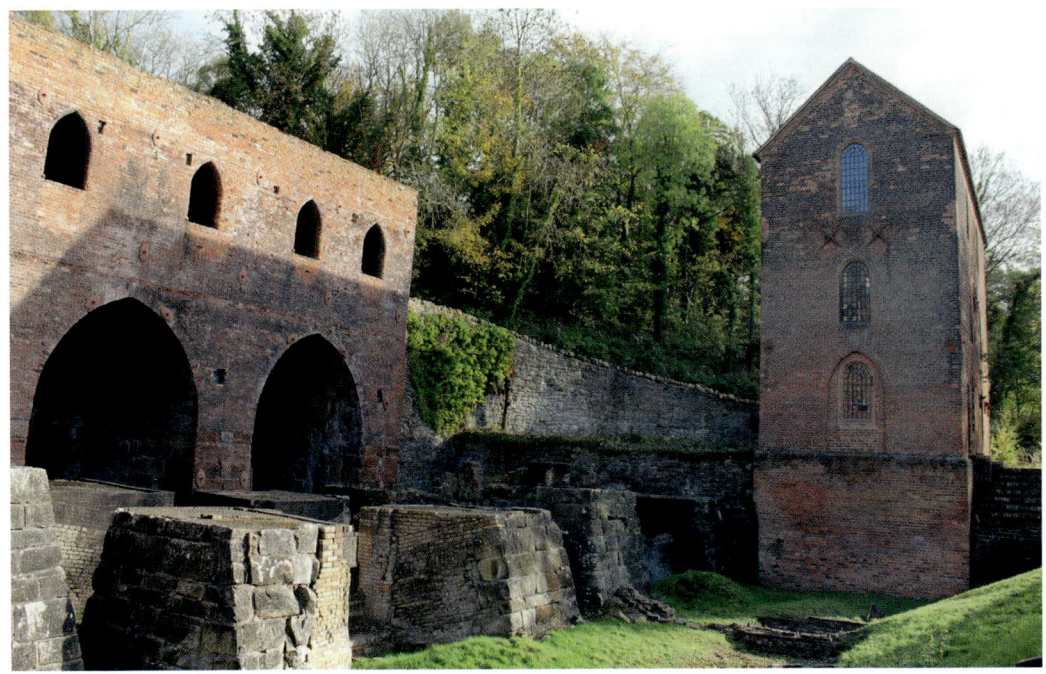

The Blists Hill furnaces in 2020 after excavation and restoration in the 1980s and 1990s. The bases for the furnaces are visible to the left of the southern engine house.

be kept in water as a reservoir in the late nineteenth century, to maintain its water supply after the canal was abandoned (Hayman Horton & White, 1999, 97–99; see Dig 3).

The two charging houses lay immediately east of the three furnaces, terraced into the hillside. Their purpose was to keep the raw materials needed for filling the furnaces, the ironstone and limestone, dry. Both were two storeys high. The northern charging house was 13 metres by 9 metres in plan and brick-built. The upper floor was supported by sandstone piers forming a tall, pointed arch in the western elevation. The southern charging house, 15 metres by 12.5 metres in plan, is larger and the upper floor is supported by four sandstone piers forming two pointed-arched vaulted chambers, strengthened by cast-iron beams. The ground floor spaces of each charging house contained a number of rooms used as workshops and smithies. The second storey in each building contained workshops, whilst above these were the charging levels to the three iron furnaces, with a series of charging bridges giving access to the top of each furnace. However, neither the charging bridges nor the form of the charging platforms survived the demolition of the furnaces (Hayman & Horton, 1999, 125–126; Hayman, Horton & White, 1999, 90–94).

The survey and excavation work in the 1990s led to the identification of four major phases of use. The first furnace to be built and used was Furnace 1 at the northern end of the range in 1832. In the period 1840–44 a new blowing engine was constructed at the southern end of the site to serve two further furnaces (numbers 2 and 3) supplied by the southern charging house. These first three blast furnaces had distinctive bottle-shaped

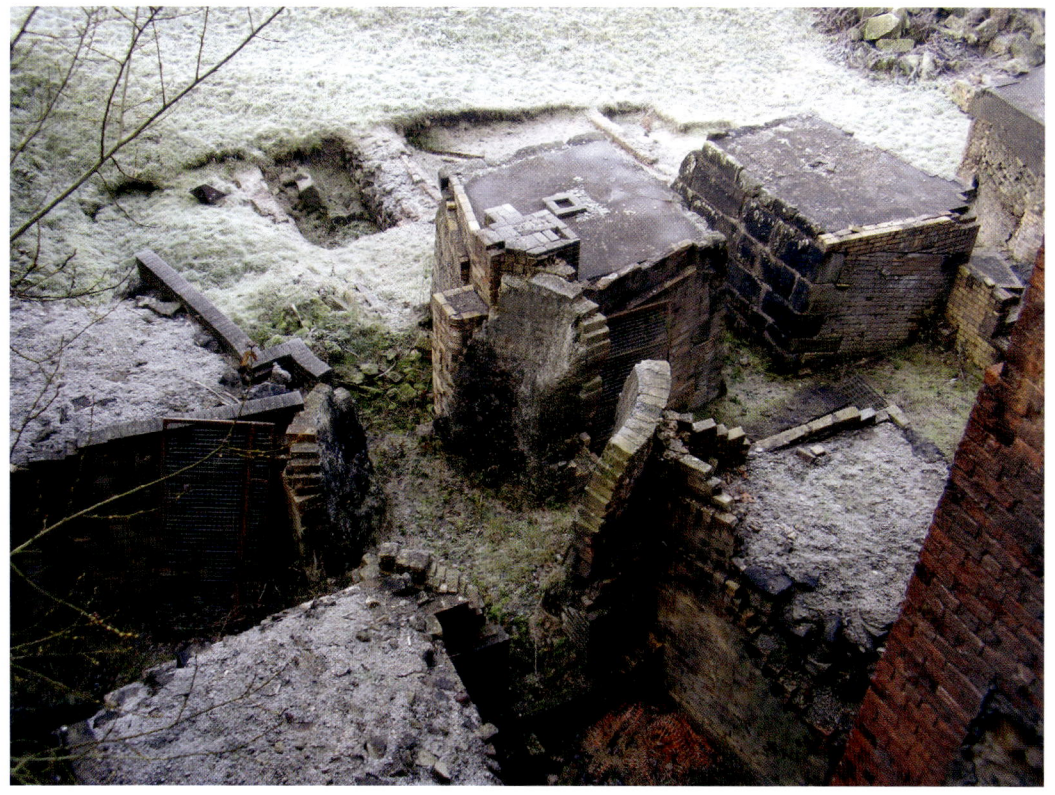

The circular base of the central blast furnace at Blists Hill in 2007. (© Ironbridge Gorge Museum Trust)

profiles, similar to the furnaces the Madeley Wood Company built at Bedlam in 1843 (see Dig 4). Between 1847 and 1871 a continuous gantry was built across the three furnaces at charging level. Then, sometime between 1871 and 1873 the furnaces were completely rebuilt to a more common cylindrical design, but using the original stone bases. These were taller than the earlier furnaces and required a higher charging level, leading to the complete rebuilding of the upper storeys of the charging houses. A lift was installed in the southern charging house for raising the ironstone and coke to the charging platform. This period also saw the construction of a calcining kiln and the rebuilding of the northern engine house. However, these new arrangements were not long in use, since 1882 was the last year that all three furnaces were used, and from 1889 only one of the new furnaces was in blast, probably number 1 (Hayman, Horton & White, 1999, 100–103).

The Blists Hill furnaces were very profitable for several decades and 11,500 tons of pig iron were produced, or roughly 30 tons per day, was produced at their peak in 1871. However, profits declined towards the end of the nineteenth century. The supply of raw materials from the nearby iron ore mine was dwindling and importing raw materials to Blists Hill was increasingly expensive, despite the arrival of the mainline railway in the 1860s. Furthermore, technology had moved on with the introduction of hot blast ironworking in the mid-nineteenth century, which preheated the air blown into the blast furnace, increasing temperatures and saving fuel. Blists Hill and the other furnaces in the Gorge used the older technique of cold blast production. When the Blists Hill coal mine closed in 1912, the last working Blists Hill blast furnace could not survive and it too was shut down (Hayman, Horton & White, 1999, 83–85).

Dig 6

Coalport China Works (1974–2003)

The Coalport China Works lies on the northern bank of the River Severn at the lower end of the Gorge, close to the southern terminus of the Shropshire Canal. Pottery kilns have been a prominent feature of the northern bank of the Severn in this area for over 200 years, their conical forms still reflected in the still waters of the canal. Industrial activity in this part of the Gorge began with the construction of the Shropshire Canal in

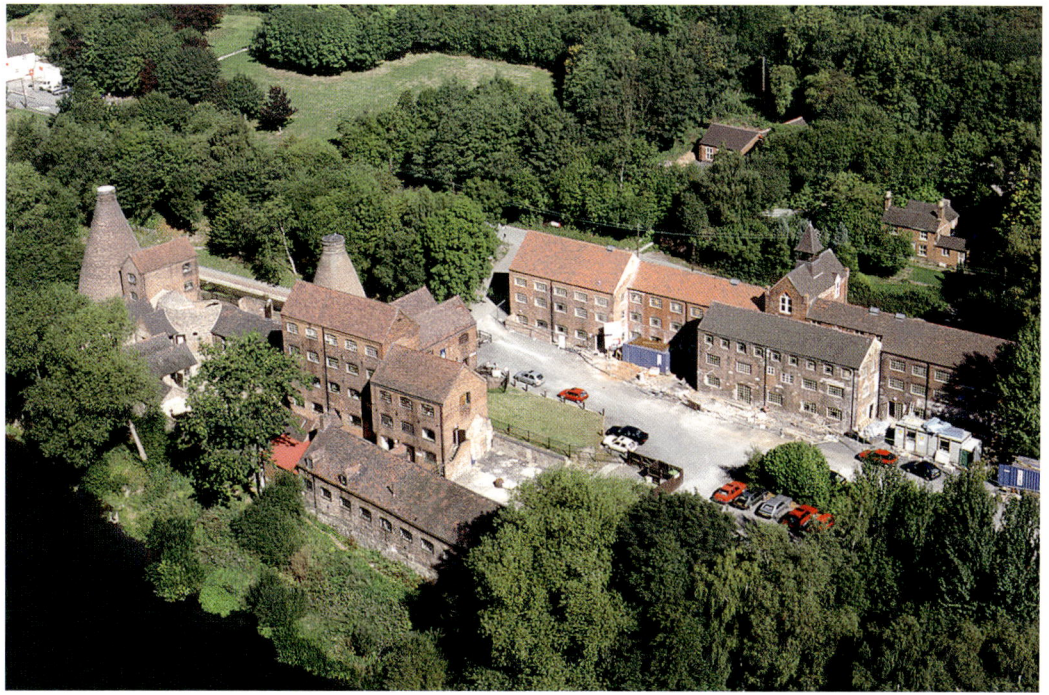

The Coalport China Works. This early twenty-first-century view shows the surviving kilns on the left, to the right of these the Cemetry Building by the river, and behind this the John Rose Building. The canal originally ran through the courtyard between these two ranges. (© Ironbridge Gorge Museum Trust)

1787 (see Dig 3). By 1794 the canal-river interchange was being referred to as Coalport (Clark, 1993, 58–63; Hayman & Horton, 1999, 75–81; Trinder, 2000, 70).

The establishment of a china pottery works at Coalport was part of the transition from the production of coarse earthenwares for a local market to the manufacture of fine pottery wares for a national market begun at the Caughley porcelain factory near Broseley. The Gorge was one of several areas in Britain that saw experiments in copying the popular blue-and-white porcelains being imported from China during the eighteenth century. The first factory to undertake such production in the Ironbridge Gorge was the Caughley Porcelain Manufactory, rebuilt by Thomas Turner in the early 1770s as a porcelain works. There were also a china works at Madeley, established in 1826 by Thomas Martin Randall, who had worked at the Caughley Porcelain Manufactory (Edmundson, 1979, 124; Hayman & Horton, 1999, 80; Trinder, 2016, 115).

The origin of the Coalport China Works, though, lies in three manufacturing sites from the period 1795–1800. In 1795 Rose and Blakeway began building the first pottery at Coalport, either a china works or a porcelain works. In 1796 Walter Bradley established an earthenware pottery works here, and a third firm was established in 1800 as Reynolds, Horton & Rose. These were gradually taken over by John Rose & Company down to 1814. John Rose also took over the Caughley Porcelain Manufactory in 1799, closing the factory in 1814 to concentrate production at Coalport. This combined factory remained in business on the site until it was bought in 1924 by Cauldron Potteries Ltd and closed in 1926, production being moved to Shelton in Staffordshire. Part of the complex was then taken over by the Nuway Rubber Mat Company, whilst other buildings on the site were occupied by a variety of metal firms into the mid-twentieth century. Several process buildings and the remains of three kilns reopened as a museum in 1976, and as part of Ironbridge Gorge Museum Trust (Barker & Horton, 1999, 5–12; Clark, 1993, 58–60).

Unlike many pottery factories from the late eighteenth and early nineteenth centuries, which were arranged around a courtyard, the works at Coalport were strung out along the canal. This made a striking industrial backdrop to the river, popular with nineteenth-century artists. Three brick-built kilns survive, each bottle-shaped and circular in plan. Two of the kilns, rebuilt around 1910, are complete while the third,

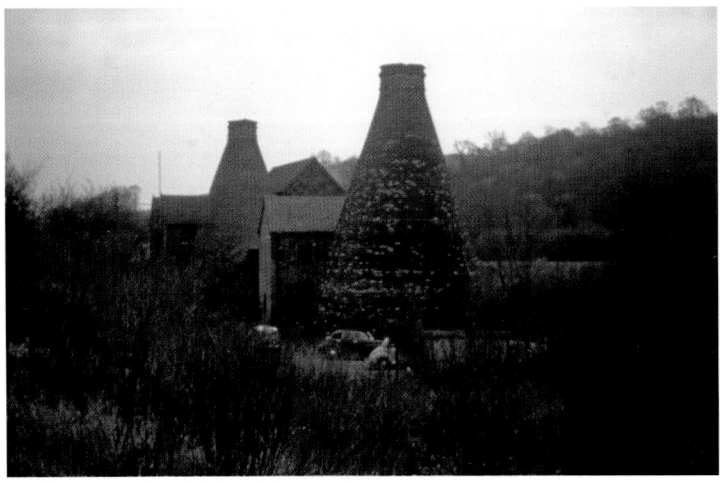

The surviving kilns at the Coalport China Works in 1965 as captured by Kate Bishop before the founding of the Ironbridge Gorge Museum Trust and before any conservation work. The Coalport Canal ran to the left of the kilns, though had long been filled by the 1960s. (© Ironbridge Gorge Museum Trust)

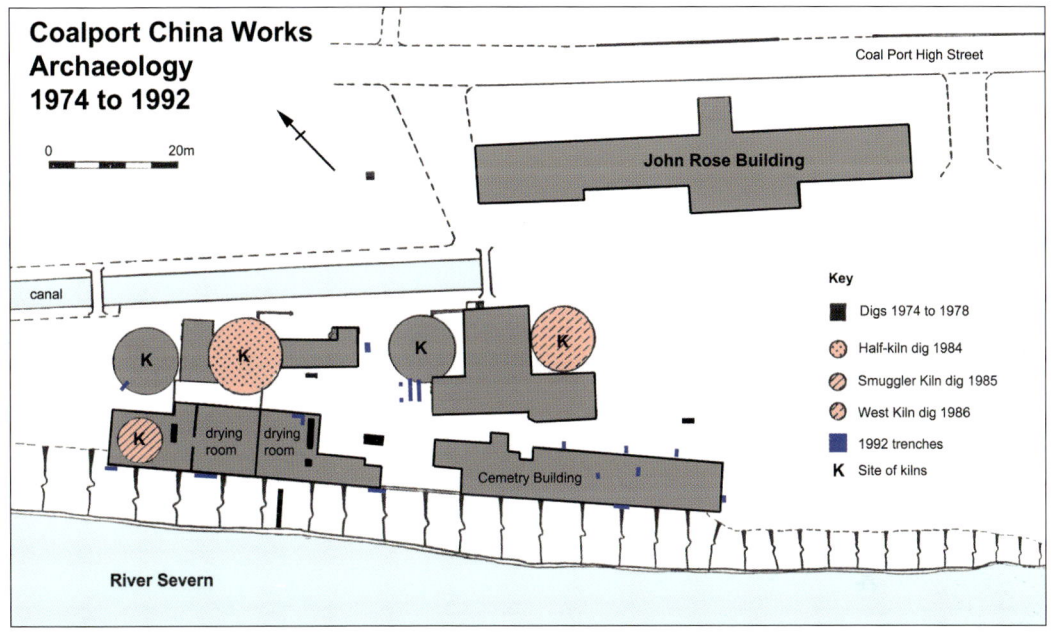

Coalport China Works Archaeology 1974 to 1992

Coal Port High Street

John Rose Building

canal

K
K
K
K
K
drying room
drying room

Cemetery Building

River Severn

Key

■ Digs 1974 to 1978
● Half-kiln dig 1984
◐ Smuggler Kiln dig 1985
◑ West Kiln dig 1986
■ 1992 trenches
K Site of kilns

0   20m

Excavation and survey plan of the Coalport China Works complex showing investigations between 1974 and 1992.

which predates 1847, is now truncated and only the lowest 5 metres remains. The adjacent and attached buildings are early nineteenth-century to early twentieth-century workshops, which housed a variety of production processes, including biscuit firing, cleaning and potting, glazing and printing. They are all brick-built structures and range from two to four storeys (Hayman & Horton, 1999, 75–80).

Excavation work at the Coalport China Works site spans the 1970s to the 2000s and was linked to the restoration of the buildings and the expansion of the museum. The first

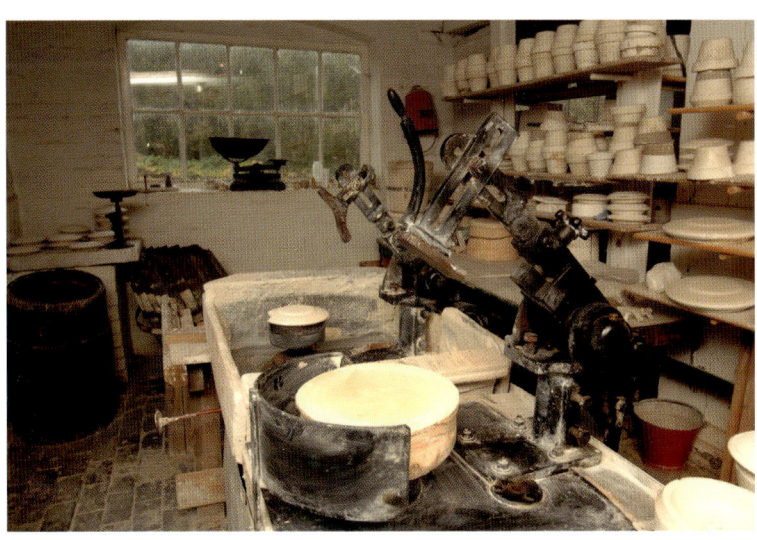

Coalport China Works interior showing surviving pottery workshop machinery. (© Ironbridge Gorge Museum Trust)

excavations on the site were undertaken by a team from the University of Manchester and the Stoke City Museum & Art Gallery for IGMT in 1974. Two of the five trenches dug produced large amounts of undisturbed nineteenth-century and early twentieth-century porcelain pottery fragments and pieces of the kiln fabric. This indicated the presence of a large nineteenth-century porcelain dump south of the canal containing pottery types manufactured by the firm of Anstice Horton & Rose (Barker and Horton, 1999, 18). The following year, 1975, the IGMT Ceramics group excavated a trench over the old Biscuit Drying Room, where stratified wasters (pottery items that had been damaged during the firing process) were located. This included deposits of earthenware pottery (creamwares and pearlwares) from the late eighteenth and early nineteenth centuries, as well as porcelain deposits. The designs ranged from teapots, tea bowls, and saucers, to bowls, mugs, jugs, tureens, and platters. This trench also indicated that the River Severn ran much closer to the canal in the nineteenth century than during the late twentieth century. In 1978 IGMT excavations extended this work to a site east of the Smuggler Kiln, recovering waster pottery fragments from the period *c*. 1795 to 1820.

The most significant excavations at the china works, at least in terms of uncovering kiln technology, were undertaken during the years 1984 to 1986. This work involved the clearance and excavation of three of the five known kiln sites. In 1984 the ruinous remains of the 'Half-Kiln', 11.73 metres in diameter, between the two intact kilns on the southern bank of the canal, was cleared of rubble and recorded in detail. The brick floor of the kiln had nine rectangular ashpits radiating from a central circular brick platform. Wedge-shaped brick piers lay between the ashpits. It was used as a biscuit kiln, like the intact kiln to the west. Firing to a biscuit state, at 1,240 degrees Celsius, meant that the goods were easier to handle and move for decoration before being later fired in the glaze kilns. The Half-Kiln appears to have collapsed in the 1950s and the name 'Half-Kiln' dates from then. Although in the twenty-first century it stands no higher than 5 metres, originally it would have stood 12.5 metres high but smaller than the two flanking surviving kilns, both of which date to around 1910. The Half-Kiln was built in the period 1814–47, making it the oldest upstanding kiln on the site. However, the excavation indicated that the kiln had been extensively rebuilt around 1902 (Trueman, 1988, 81–86). In 1978 and again

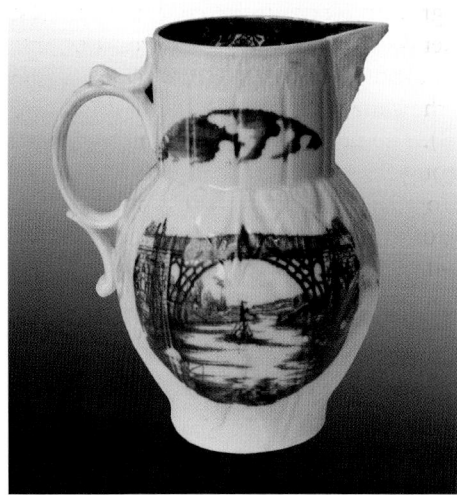

A nineteenth-century jug manufactured at Coalport with an Iron Bridge print on the body. (© Ironbridge Gorge Museum Trust)

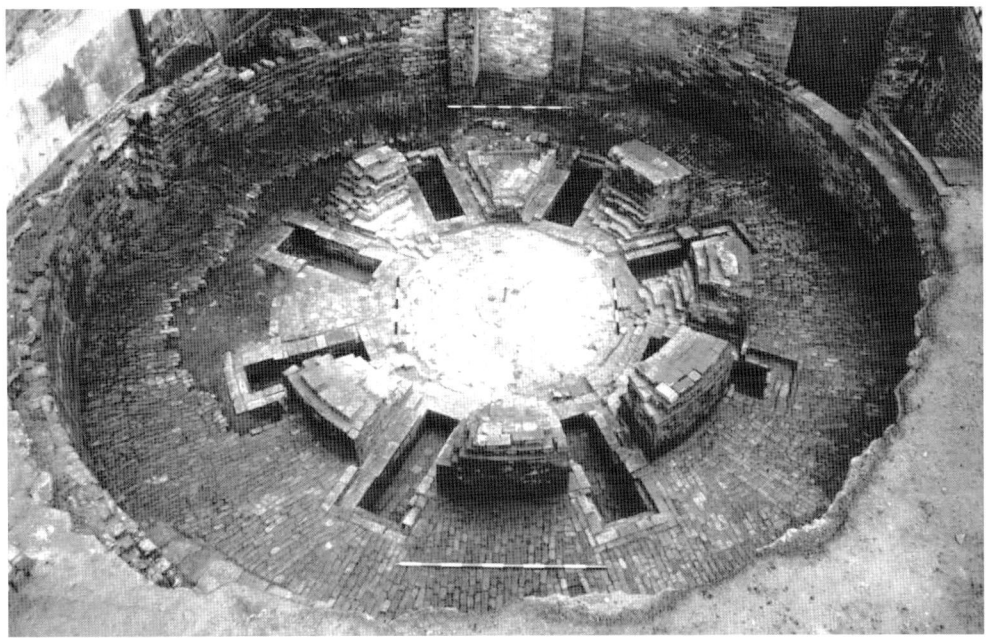

The foundations of the West Kiln, as exposed during excavation in 1986. (© Ironbridge Gorge Museum Trust)

in 1985 the foundations of the Smuggler Kiln, another biscuit kiln of smaller diameter, were cleared and recorded in a museum building to the west of the Half-Kiln and south of the saggar store. This kiln dated to the period 1814–47, like the Half-Kiln. Immediately to the east lay biscuit-drying rooms, where stoves were used for drying the pottery before the first firing in the biscuit kilns. In 1986 the foundations of the West Kiln, which confusingly lay east of the museum buildings, were completely stripped. This structure was found to have eight fireboxes and an entrance to the north (Clark & Alfrey, 1986, 57–76).

Repair works throughout the 1990s and into the 2000s gave opportunities to undertake further excavation of the below ground deposits around the process buildings, and to record the process buildings themselves. Thus, drainage work in 1992 revealed later nineteenth-century pottery dumps around the wharf south of the canal and around the Cemetry Building. Work along the canal through the site in 2003 also revealed the limits of the pottery dumps (Dig 13). The pottery wasters from more than thirty trenches reflected the fabrics and styles found in the 1970s and 1980s trenches and confirmed that pottery waste occurred across the site (Barker & Horton, 1999, 18–28; Horton, Richardson, White & Worthington, 1993).

The excavations over three decades at the Coalport China Works have produced the best evidence for pottery production in the Gorge. The extensive range of products recorded is significant not just for Ironbridge and the West Midlands, but for archaeological studies throughout Britain and across the trade networks of the British Empire. Their presence beyond the Gorge in archaeological deposits is a valuable dating tool (Hayman & Horton, 1999, 75–80). Furthermore, these products are a reminder of the national and international trade links of the Gorge during the late eighteenth century and throughout the nineteenth century.

Dig 7

Jackfield Tile Works (1981–2012)

There are over thirty brick, roofing tile, and decorative tile manufacturing sites known in the Gorge. The village of Jackfield on the southern bank of the River Severn has one of the longest histories of manufacture in the area, going back to at least 1723 with the start of the production of roof tiles. These ceramic industries reached their

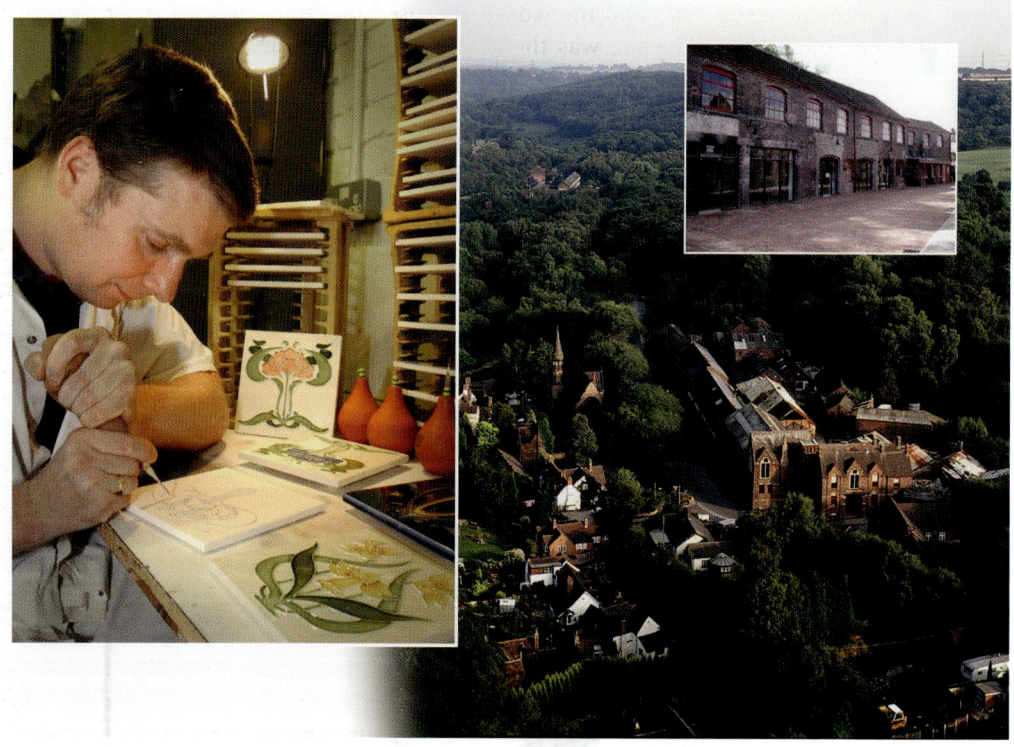

The Jackfield Tile Works complex in the early twenty-first century. Tile manufacture continues at the site, which was established in the 1874 by Craven Dunnill & Co. (© Ironbridge Gorge Museum Trust)

peak with the establishment in the later nineteenth century of two encaustic/decorative tile works: that of Maws & Co. in 1862 and Hargreaves, Craven, Dunnill & Co. in 1870. Arthur and George Maw brought encaustic/decorative tile production to the valley when they moved their Worcester factory to Broseley. Here, encaustic tiles were produced using a technique where layers of different coloured clay were used to create elaborate, colourful and, importantly, durable designs. In 1883 they moved the company to the newly built Benthall Works in Jackfield. Hargreaves, Craven, Dunnill & Co. became Craven Dunnill & Co. in 1872 and in 1874 they built a new factory at Jackfield, designed by the Stoke-on-Trent architect Charles Lynam, now the Jackfield Tile Museum. Both companies developed worldwide reputations for their decorative floor and wall tiles (Baggs et al, 1998, 273–276).

The 1874 works of Craven Dunnill & Co. survives largely intact. Originally it comprised four bottle-shaped kilns, a mosaic workshop, a drying house, a mill building, clay arks, two warehouses, one stable, a gasworks, and a trade showroom for buyers. These buildings were set around a courtyard and occupied *c.* 0.75ha of land along the southern bank of the River Severn. The two-storey road frontage with its prominent white company signage and row of forty windows runs for over 100 metres and originally had railway sidings along its length. Craven Dunnill & Co. employed just under a hundred people. Women were employed widely throughout the production process, forming up to a third of the workforce on both the factory floor and in the offices. The firm closed their Jackfield site in 1952 and the works was used by Osbourne & Co. Ltd, precision engineers, until 1982. The site was then taken over by the Ironbridge Gorge Museum Trust and opened as a tile museum in 1984 (Baggs et al, 1998, 275). However, in 2000 the Craven Dunnill group of companies returned to the Jackfield museum site to resume the production of encaustic tiles once more within the complex, and in 2022 are still manufacturing on part of the site using some of the historic nineteenth-century machinery.

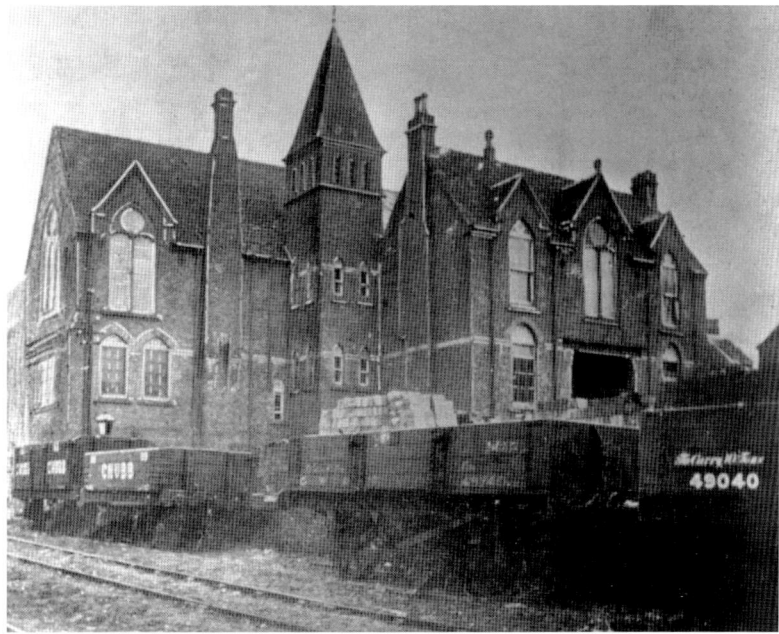

The western end of the works, showing the main entrance in the 1900s and the railway sidings used by the tile works. (© Ironbridge Gorge Museum Trust)

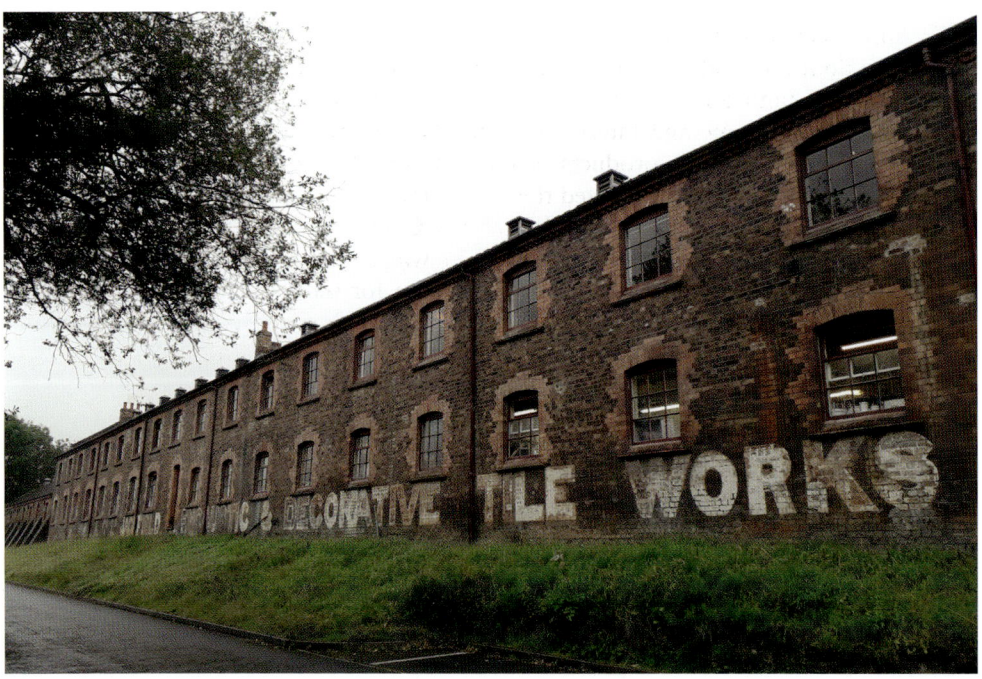

The road frontage of the two-storey Jackfield Tile Works with its prominent white company signage and row of forty windows.

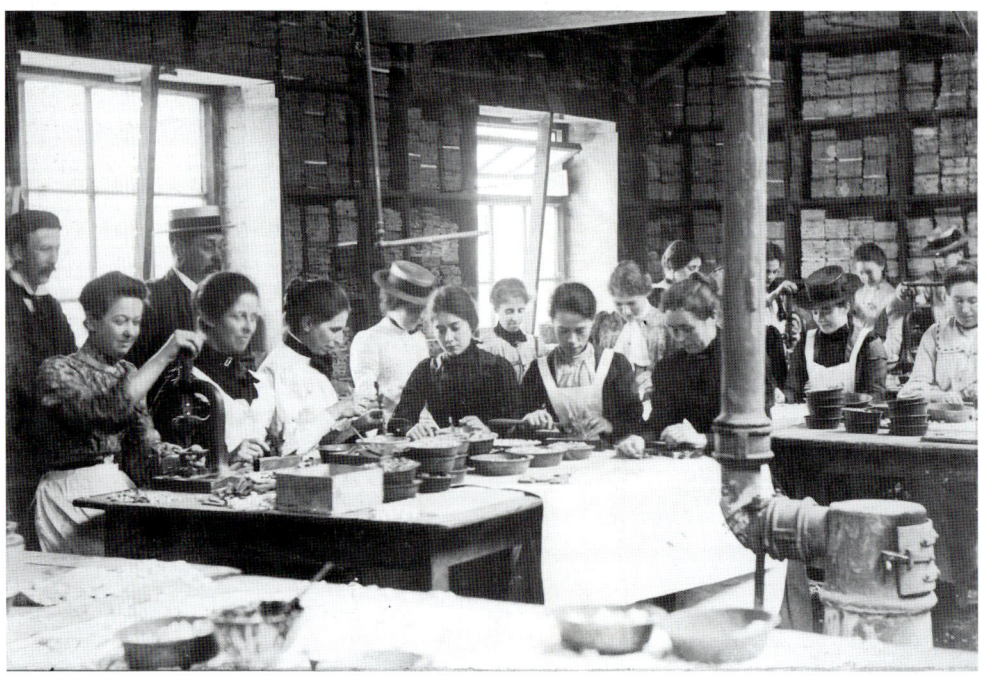

Female workers in the Mosaic Shop at Jackfield around 1900. Over a third of the workforce at this date were women. (© Ironbridge Gorge Museum Trust)

The products manufactured on the site from 1874 to 1952 ranged from highly decorative floor tiles and the thinner and shinier wall tiles to the cheaper transfer-printed tiles, for use in both domestic, hospital, public house, office, and retail settings. These were sold in both home and international markets. Craven Dunnill & Co. also made 'Art Pottery', more artistic products inspired by the Arts and Crafts movement. The Great Exhibition in 1851 highlighted the poor quality of much British design compared to other countries in Europe and North America. Consequently, in 1856 the Science and Art Department, part of the Board of Education, was set up. Based in South Kensington, London, it allocated grants and set the curriculum for schools of art. This led to the establishment of 675 art schools across England by 1880, including the Coalbrookdale School of Art, established in 1853 (Grant & Crumpton, 2020, 2–3).

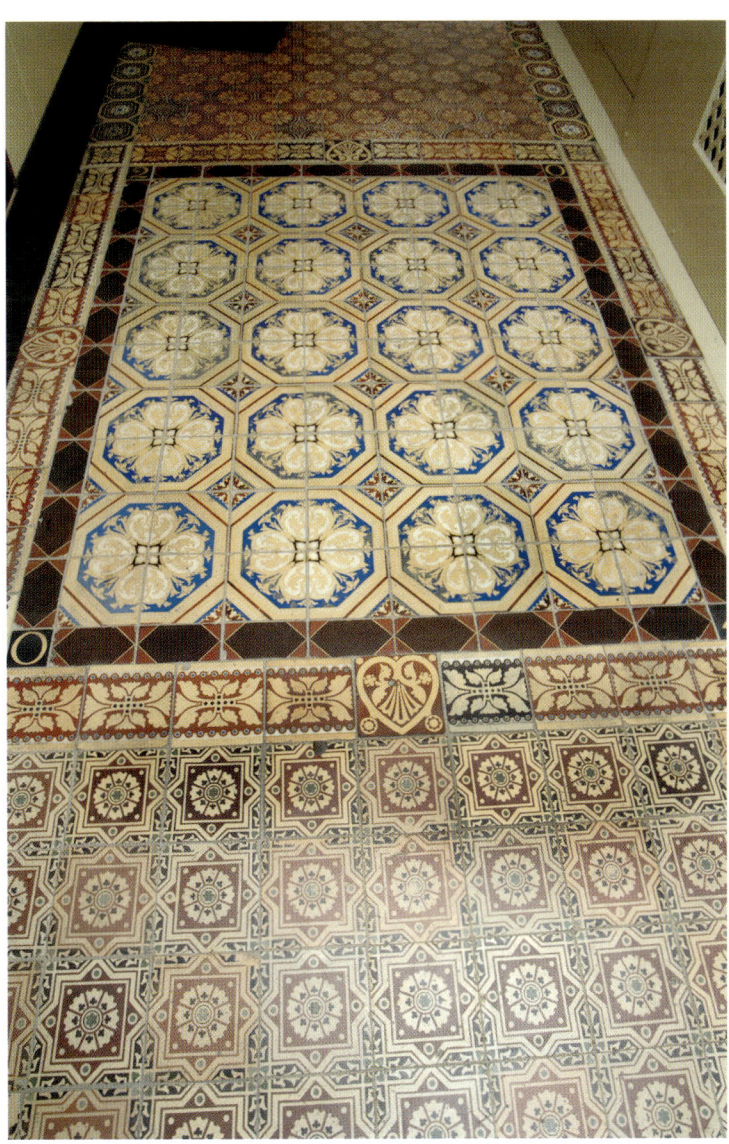

An 1870s encaustic tile floor at the Jackfield Tile Works with designs typical of the period. (© Ironbridge Gorge Museum Trust)

Thus, the rise of design as a central part of the production process developed in the second half of the nineteenth century to improve the quality of design in manufacturing industry, as well as the broader arts. Companies such as Craven Dunnill & Co. had their own design studio and used their own inhouse designers to produce their main range of tile and industrial products. However, they also employed independent designers, who could be well known nationally, such as Walter Crane, who designed book illustrations and fabrics. For Craven Dunnill & Co. he designed a set of vases based upon ancient Greek myths and Icelandic sagas.

Most of the production buildings now form part of the museum and house a large collection of decorative tiles from both Craven Dunnill & Co. and Maws & Co., as well as other manufacturers from outside the Gorge. From 1981 to 1986 archaeological work was undertaken at the western end of the Craven Dunnill & Co. site on an early bottle-shaped pottery kiln predating the tile works, and on the site of two down-draught kilns built for the tile works. Archaeological trenching across part of the site in 1997 suggested the location of further, pre-tileworks pottery kilns probably associated with the Ash Tree pottery. Excavation on one of these kilns sites was undertaken in 2001, recovering tile and kiln fabric (Trueman, 1988).

Further survey work from 2002 to 2006 recorded the standing buildings and excavated part of the Foundry Building revealing the base of Kiln 4 and re-excavated the earlier kiln located in 1983. This worked allowed a reinterpretation of the processes undertaken in the Drying House and Mill Buildings, which both lay at the eastern end of the site (Belford, 2009b). Small-scale work in 2012 uncovered the previously excavated foundation of Kiln 4. Since little documentary history for the business development of the site survives, this archaeological work is an important way of uncovering the story of the works and the people who manufactured and decorated the tiles.

Dig 8

Excavation and Survey along The Wharfage (1983–88)

The river frontage known as The Wharfage in Ironbridge is one of the most recognisable features of the Gorge. A walk eastwards through this area in the twenty-first century takes the visitor along a rising embankment on the northern side of the river, past restaurants, guest houses, and shops, towards the Iron Bridge. Many of the buildings along this river frontage hide an industrial past, for in the seventeenth, eighteenth, and nineteenth centuries this area was just one part of a wider transport zone connecting the river and the industries to the north by road, railway, and canal routes. A similar transhipment area lay on the opposite, southern bank of the Severn (Alfrey & Clark, 1993, 136–137). This bustling waterfront was used for both the short-term storage of raw materials and finished goods, as well as the transfer of products from the coal mines, ironworks, and limestone quarries that lay on either side of the river, making it the transport heart of industrial Ironbridge.

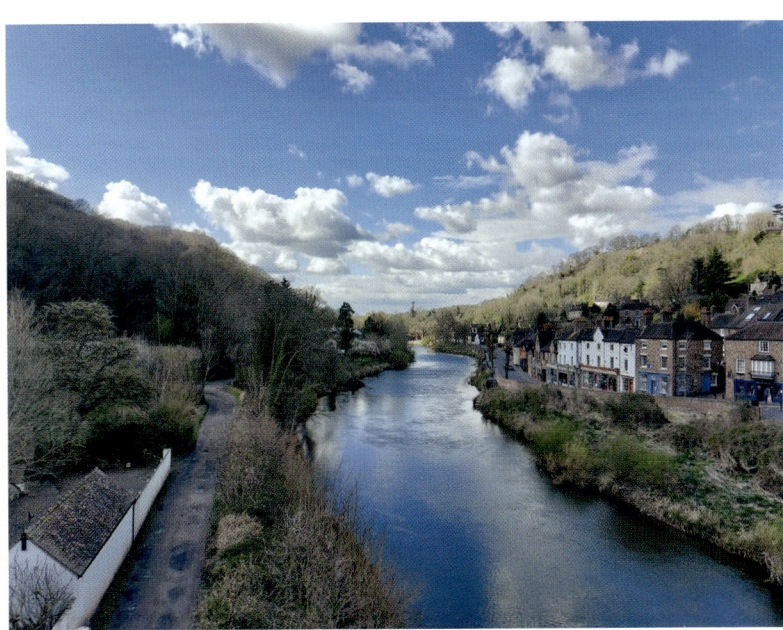

The Wharfage area along the northern bank of the River Severn at Ironbridge in 2022 viewed from the Iron Bridge. The Severn Warehouse can be seen in the far distance.

Survey work and excavation during the period 1983–88 of the buildings along The Wharfage revealed how extensive such storage facilities and secondary industries were (Trueman, 1986 and 1988). This work included from west to east, the Severn Warehouse on the southern side of The Wharfage by the river, and along the northern side of the road, Nos 23 and 22 The Wharfage, the Swan Hotel, No. 20 The Wharfage, and excavation work on the adjacent limekilns.

The most visible industrial building in this group is the present Museum of the Gorge, formerly the Severn Warehouse. This was erected by the Coalbrookdale Company in

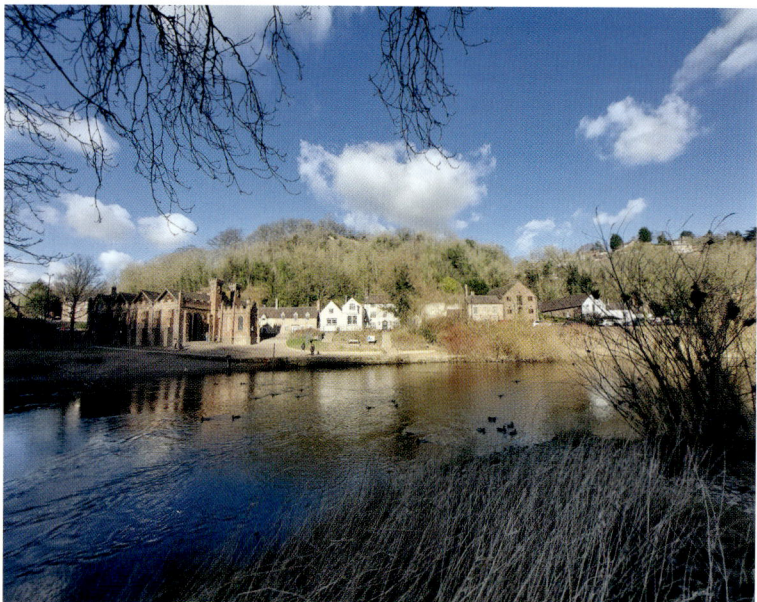

The buildings at western end of The Wharfage, with from left to right: the Severn Warehouse, the two-storey brick workers' cottages forming Nos 23 and 24, the white-painted frontage of the Swan Inn and its warehouse, and on the right the tall brown gable of No. 20, a warehouse with loading doors.

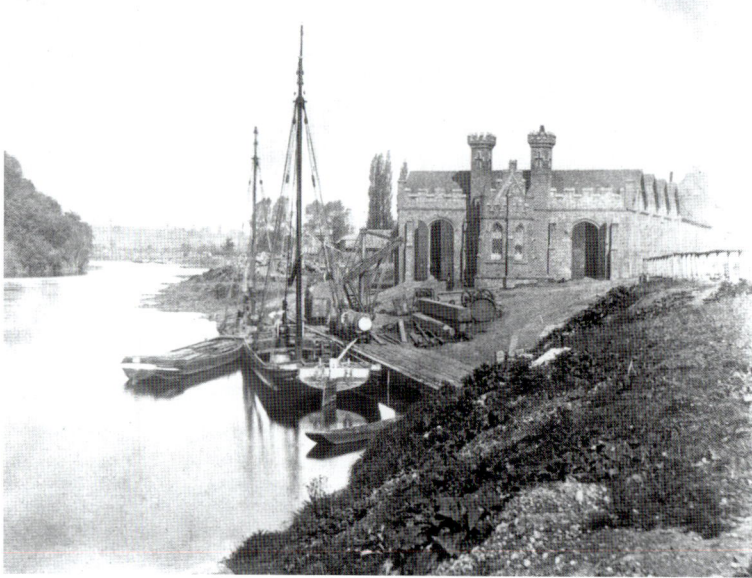

A late nineteenth-century view of the Severn Warehouse with a trow tied to the quay ready for loading from the railway trucks on the bank. (© Ironbridge Gorge Museum Trust)

1834 to a design by Samuel Cookson (Newman & Pevsner, 2006, 634). The building was purchased in 1974 by Telford Development Corporation and restored by the Ironbridge Gorge Museum Trust as a visitor centre, opening in 1977. It is a striking Gothic-style single-storey building with lancet windows, buttresses, and two castellated turrets between which is a castellated apse. It was used as a warehouse for goods from the barges that tied up on the adjacent quay, and a cart entrance can still be seen on the northern roadside elevation. A network of railways brought finished iron products both through the building and down to the quayside from the company's works at Coalbrookdale for transhipment onto the river.

Opposite and east of this warehouse lie Nos 23 and 22 The Wharfage, a set of late eighteenth- and nineteenth-century cottages. Surveyed in 1988, No. 22 is a late eighteenth-century two-storey brick cottage, two rooms wide (Winkworth, 1988). To the west lies a two-storey house, No. 23, originally a row of three brick-built cottages. Built piecemeal, the easternmost bay, comprising just two rooms, may have begun as an addition to No. 23. Two further rooms to the west were added by the mid-nineteenth century, along with a rear wing. The whole complex was converted into a single dwelling by the end of the century. Such buildings, squeezed into the hillside and extended on numerous occasions, reflect both the demand for new building land in nineteenth-century Ironbridge, and the modest scale of early workers' housing within the Gorge.

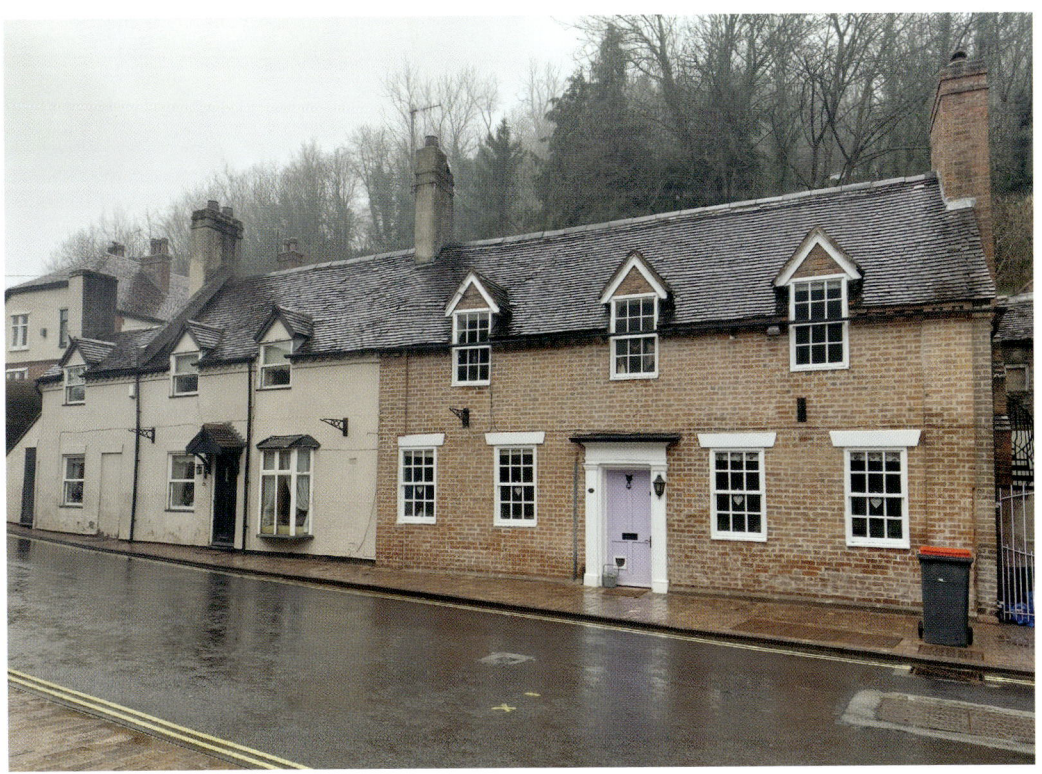

The late eighteenth- and nineteenth-century workers' cottages forming Nos 23 and 24 The Wharfage.

Beyond these cottages is the L-shaped courtyard complex known in the twenty-first century as the Swan Hotel. The site is terraced into the hillside and probably began as cottages in the late seventeenth or early eighteenth century. Documentary evidence shows that that the two-storey eastern range was converted during the 1760s into an inn, whilst a three-storey brick malthouse building with cellar was added to the west. Maltings were kiln structures used to artificially germinate grain (usually barley) and then stop it as particular point in order to conserve the sugars contained within the budding grain. This malted grain was then dried in a kiln and used in the brewing process (Palmer, Nevell & Sissons, 2012, 61–64). The malting structures at the Swan were recorded in detail by Ironbridge archaeologists in 1986. The malt house, where the grain was germinated, had two major phases, the eastern bay being a late eighteenth-century addition, complete with a roof structure that reused cruck trusses. The original kiln lay at the northern end of the western bay, but this was replaced by a larger square stone-built kiln structure with a louvered roof in the early nineteenth century. The kiln and malthouse may have been in use as late as 1946 and are the only complete set of maltings to survive in the Gorge (Terry, 1988).

East of the Swan Hotel is No. 20 The Wharfage. This is an early to mid-nineteenth-century, three-storey, brick-built warehouse. Its southern gable faces the road and contains three loading bays, whilst the main axis of the building runs northwards into the hillside. A small two-storey house-cum-office abuts the western wall of the warehouse.

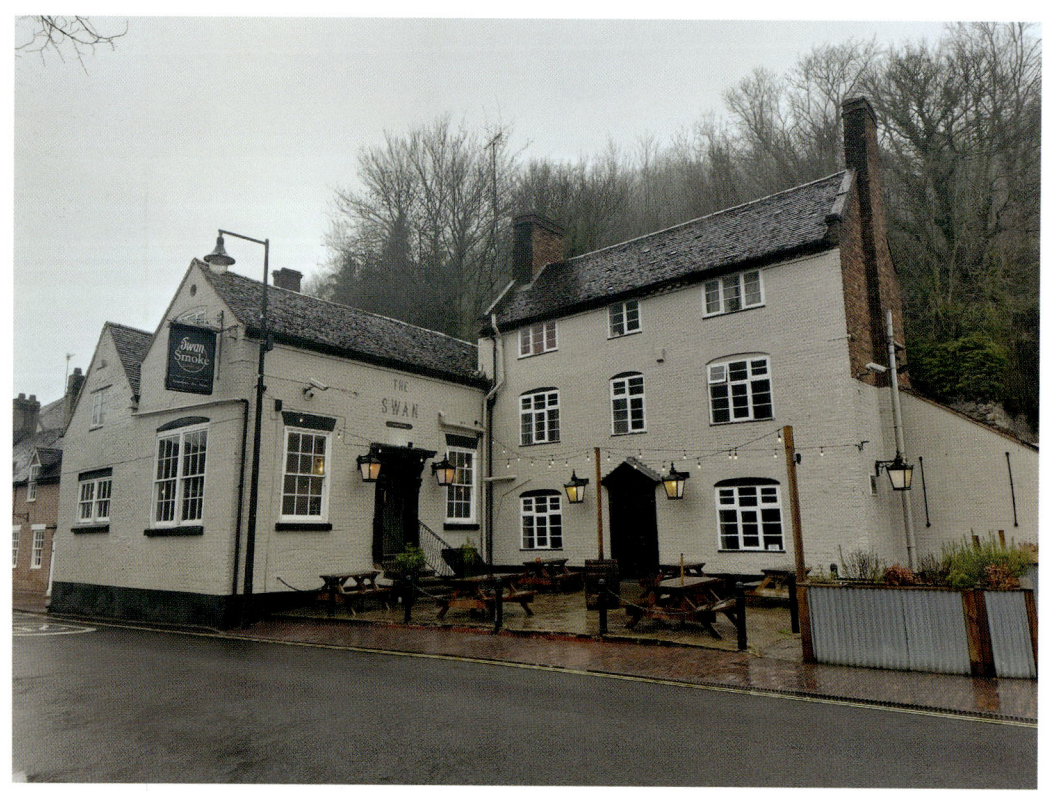

The eighteenth-century Swan Inn and, to the left, the former malthouse.

Immediately to the east of this building lies the remains of three limekilns (Hayman & Horton, 1999, 120). Limekilns were used to heat limestone, changing its chemical composition, and turning the blocks of stone into a powder (Palmer, Nevell & Sissons, 2012, 120–123). This powder was used in the construction industry (in mortar and cement), and as a fertilizer to improve soil. There are dozens of limekilns along the Gorge, mostly on the southern side of the river. One of these limekilns was investigated through excavation and survey in 1985, ahead of building work, revealing the lower third of the kiln (Trueman, 1986). The limekiln had an inner chamber, or pot, shaped like an inverted cone, which was lined with a double thickness of brick. This would have been filled or charged with alternate layers of limestone and coal for fuel from the top of the kiln, which was terraced into the hillside. When excavated the chamber still contained the last charge of mixed coal and limestone at its base. The three limekilns were in use from around 1760 to 1870, the limestone coming from Lincoln Hill, which lies behind and to the north of the site. Joseph Turner visited the area and painted these limekilns in 1796.

Together, the conservation of these cottages, warehouses, and structures relating to secondary industries such as lime burning, malting, and storage are a reminder of the former commercial bustle of The Wharfage zone along the northern bank of the River Severn.

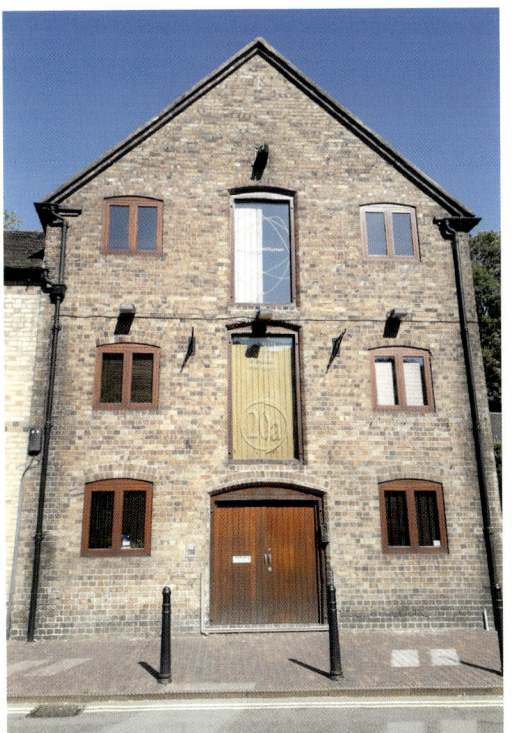

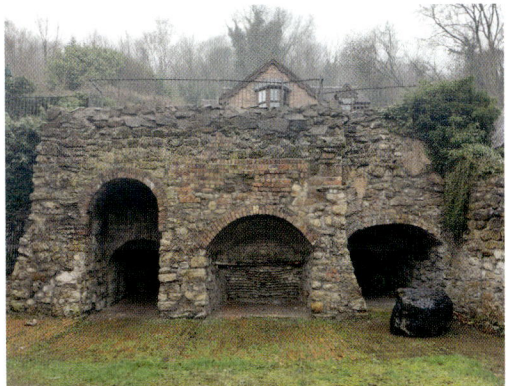

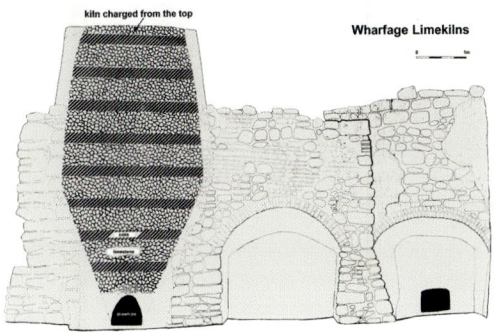

Above left: The gable of No. 20 The Wharfage, a nineteenth-century warehouse typical of many still to be found along The Wharfage riverfront.

Above right: The eighteenth- and nineteenth-century limekilns east of No. 20 The Wharfage. These lie at the foot of Lincoln Hill, which was extensively quarried for its limestone.

Dig 9

Blists Hill Mine (1982–93)

Deep coal mining in the Severn Gorge dates to at least the seventeenth century when horizontal tunnels or adits were dug into the valley sides in search of coal, whilst the digging of surface coal goes back even further to the late medieval period. The first steam-powered colliery pumping engine on the Shropshire coalfield was erected at The Lloyds in Madeley in 1719 (Dig 14), just seven years after Thomas Newcomen patented his steam-powered water pumping engine. A visitor to the Gorge in 1768 noted that the Coalbrookdale Company alone had six colliery pumping engines at work in their mines along the valley (Hayman & Horton, 1999, 53–54; Palmer, Nevell & Sissons, 2012, 97; Trinder, 2016, 108–109; Trinder, 2017, 41–42).

The Blists Hill area was used from the late eighteenth century down to the first half of the twentieth century for mining coal and clay, and for brick, tile, and drainage pipe manufacture. The first coal shafts were dug here by ironmaster William Reynolds in the mid-1780s and lay to the west of the later canal. These shafts, which were sunk to a depth of 183 metres, were connected to the Tar Tunnel (Dig 2). The mine was expanded by the Madeley Wood Company and in the mid-nineteenth century was supplying coal and ironstone to the nearby furnaces.

The remains of a late eighteenth century pumping engine house at Blists Hill were identified and excavated in 1982 and 1984. A prominent feature of the Blists Hill site

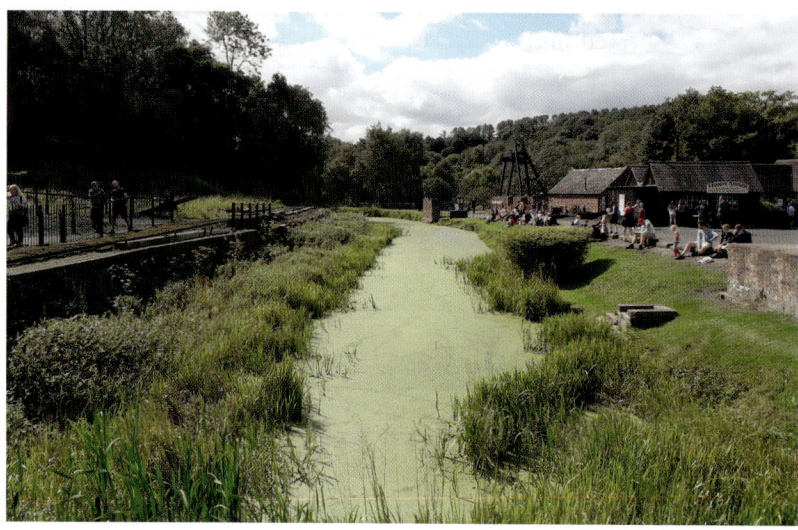

The Shropshire Canal at Blists Hill in 2022 looking south towards the Blists Hill Mines. which lie to the right of the canal.

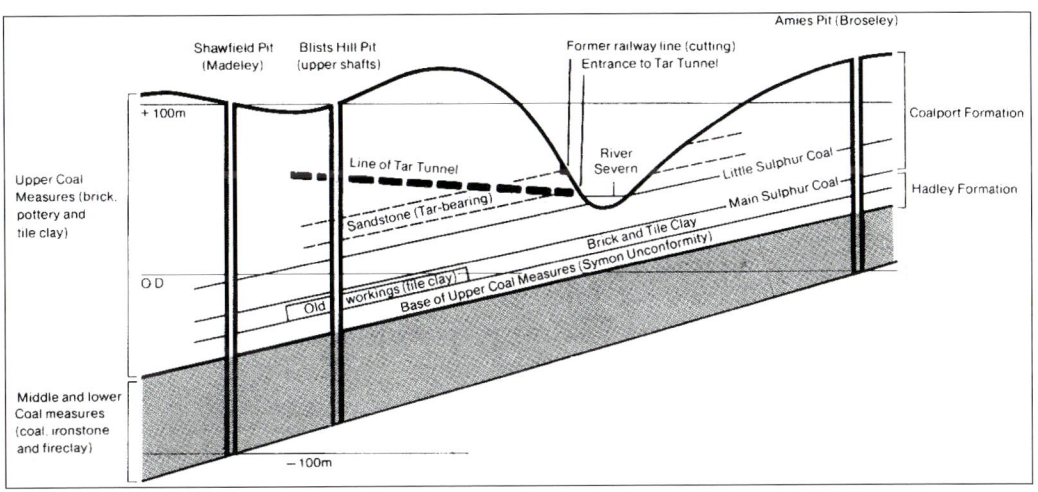

A section through the geology of the Blists Hill landscape showing the location of the mine shafts and the Tar Tunnel. (© Ironbridge Gorge Museum Trust)

in the twenty-first century is the replica wooden headgear west of the canal and above one of the two original mine shafts operated by the Blists Hill Pit. The small brick winding house next door is a reconstruction on its original site but the winding engine it contains came from the Milburgh Tileries in Jackfield. The second mine shaft lies in the allotments to south of the replica headgear, and it was here that the first winding engine was built to pump water out of the deep mine in the 1790s.

Blists Hill Pit is notable in the development of mining technology as one of the places where the steam winding of coal was developed. Here, William Reynolds employed Adam Heslop to design a winding engine for the mine sunk in the 1780s (Trinder, 2008, 21–22). This engine was not the standard pumping engine of the period, but rather an innovative setup using two cylinders instead of the normal one cylinder. Designed by Heslop, this type of engine had a cylinder at each end of the beam, one being a single-acting steam-powered cylinder, the other working like those seen on the early atmospheric engines designed by Thomas Newcomen. Heslop served his apprenticeship at the Madeley Wood Company

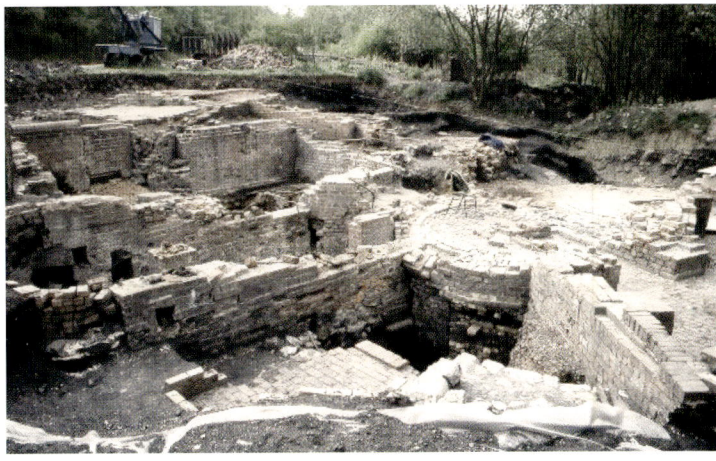

The excavation of the Blists Hill 1790s mine pumping engine in 1984. The circular boiler base can be seen on the right. (© Ironbridge Gorge Museum Trust)

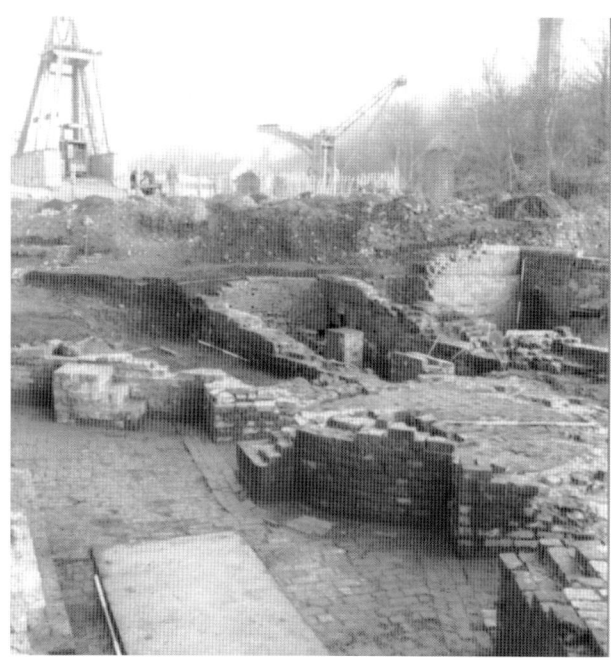

The excavation of the Blists Hill 1790s mine pumping engine in 1984, with the restored mine headgear in the background. To the right the chimney for the boilers at the Madeley Wood Brick and Tile Works can be seen on the opposite side of the canal. (© Ironbridge Gorge Museum Trust)

and patented his engine design in 1790, whilst still working for them. The Blists Hill Mine engine was erected soon after. The company manufactured and used several of these engines after Heslop had left (see Dig 3) and were still running three such engines in the early twentieth century at their mines (Brown 1991, 8; Raistrick, 1953, 57; Trinder, 2000, 49). A description of the two mine engines at Blists Hill, including the Heslop engine, survives from 1912. This describes the engine as having two cylinders of 35 inches (0.89 metres) and 24 inches (0.61 metres) in diameter, a 14-foot- (4.3-metre-) long beam and a flywheel 13 feet (4 metres) in diameter. The adjacent surviving cast-iron haystack boiler was 10 feet (3 metres) by 12 feet (3.6 metres) (Leese, 1912).

In 1982 a group of volunteers from the Ryton Hall School near Shifnal investigated, with the help of Ironbridge archaeologists, the extent of surviving below-ground remains of the Heslop engine site. A single trench, 7 metres by 3.5 metres, was dug and demolition rubble, clay, and coal waste removed to depth of 0.75 metres to 1 metre. Beneath were located the brick walls and floor of building, although these were not excavated. In December 1984 Ironbridge archaeologists returned to the site ahead of a planned museum expansion, stripping a large area of roughly 25 metres by 30 metres to reveal the complete plan of two engine houses and their boilers, and confirming that the earlier engine house was the site of the 1790s Heslop steam engine. It was then back-filled. Further small-scale archaeological work was undertaken around the engine house in 1993 as part of the capping of the two mine shafts on the site (Clark & Alfrey, 1986, 41; Truman, 1986, 35–54; Worthington, 1993).

This work revealed three main phases of activity. The earliest was represented by the remains of the Heslop pumping engine house and an associated circular haystack boiler. The engine house was a rectangular brick-built structure, 7 metres by 3.5 metres, with 0.5-metre-thick walls standing over 1 metre high in places with a curved northern wall. A fragment of steam pipework survived at the northern end of the structure along with

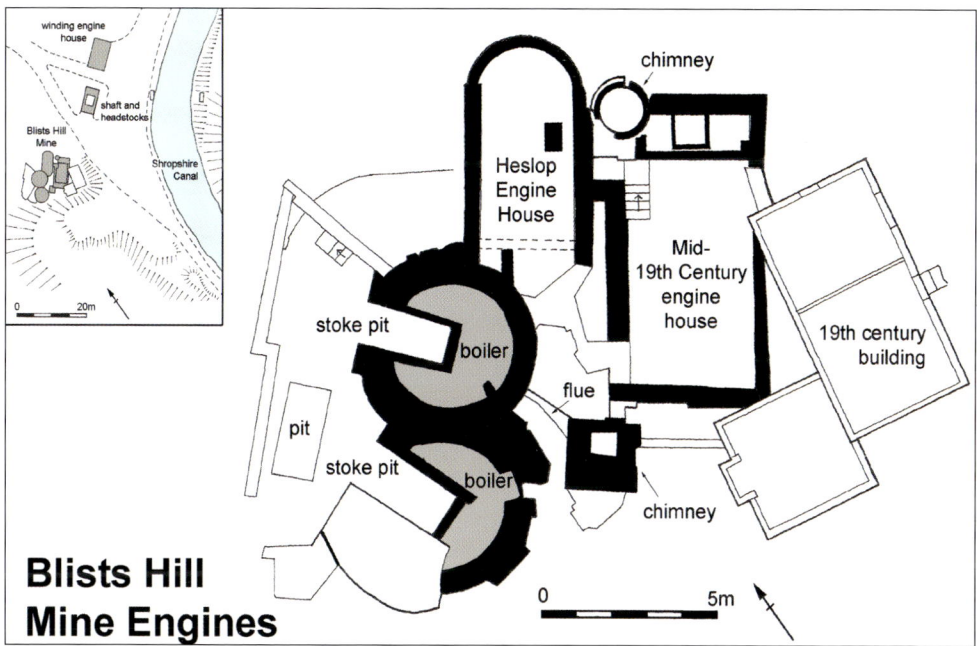

Excavation plan from 1984 of the 1790s Blists Hill pumping engine complex.

two machine bases, which may mark the location of the 'hot' or receiving cylinder. The second, cold cylinder would lie at the other end of the beam, probably outside the engine house, the engine house wall possibly acting as the support for the beam. However, the precise arrangement of the engine remained unclear. Immediately to the south-west of the engine house was the circular brick base of a contemporary haystack boiler, 5.1 metres in diameter, which supplied the steam for the cylinders. This boiler had a rectangular stoking pit 2.9 metres long and 1.7 metres wide on its western side (Worthington, 1993).

A second, mid-nineteenth century, engine house abutted the eastern side of the first engine. This structure was 4.7 metres wide and 8.4 metres long and in places the brick walls still stood nearly 2 metres high. Steam for this engine came from a second haystack boiler, *c.* 5 metres in diameter, south of the first. The pipework bringing the steam to the newer engine survived at the southern end of the structure, whilst the square-sectioned chimney for the waste gases lay between the haystack boilers and the later engine house. At the northern end of the complex was a short stretch of railway, either late eighteenth or early nineteenth century in date, used to bring coal to heat the boilers. A brick-lined mine shaft, 2 metres (6 feet 6 inches) square, lay roughly 8 metres to the north of the engine houses (Clark, 1993, 33; Trueman, 1985, 38–54; Worthington, 1993).

These two engines appear to have worked in conjunction during the later nineteenth century and were described as still in use by Leese in 1912. However, shortly afterwards this part of the Blists Hill Mine complex was closed, and the buildings demolished by the 1920s, only to be rediscovered and excavated in the 1980s. The site of the Heslop engine is one of only a handful of eighteenth-century colliery pumping or winding engines that have been excavated in Britain, making this yet another nationally important archaeological site within the Gorge (George & Nevell, 2014).

Dig 10

Newdale Industrial Settlement (1987)

Newdale was a planned industrial ironworking hamlet built by the Coalbrookdale Company in 1759 in the township of Lawley. Located 5 kilometres north of the old furnace site, this new industrial settlement comprised a furnace, a forge, a steam engine, workers' housing, and a school. The industrial hamlet was linked to Horsehay by a horse-drawn railway and the intention appears to have been to use the local coal deposits to fuel the ironworks.

Ironworking did not survive long at Newdale and had ceased by 1768, the year in which one process building was converted into a Quaker meeting house. This sudden reversal after so much expense by the company was in part a result of Abraham Darby II winning in 1762 a drawn-out Chancery case against John Wilkinson and others, who had tried to buy out half of the Coalbrookdale Works in 1757 (Thomas, 2001, unpublished IGMT research paper). Fearing defeat, Darby was proposing to abandon the site and create a new works up at Newdale. The community, however, lived on, turning to coal mining and later agriculture. The two ironworking buildings were converted into a Quaker meeting house and a domestic dwelling and were later used as a Methodist chapel and a barn. By 1861, 230 people were living in the settlement, with the census returns of that year giving mining as the chief occupation, although there were also stonemasons and forgemen listed. Coal mining continued in this area into the twentieth century, but in 1910 Newdale was sold in several lots by the Coalbrookdale Company. Thereafter, the community focussed on farming, but gradually the buildings became run down and a number abandoned. Most of the mid-eighteenth-century structures were still standing in the 1960s, when Telford New Town demolished some of the housing as part of their slum clearance programme (Horton, Clark, Trinder & Cox, 1992).

In 1987 detailed archaeological work was undertaken ahead of open-cast coal mining and landscaping across the site. This was the largest excavation undertaken in the Coalbrookdale landscape up to this date. A team of IGMT archaeologists worked on the site from July to November of that year. The two main industrial structures, the North and South buildings, were still standing, allowing detailed building recorded to be undertaken, and excavation of the interior floors.

The North Building was a rectangular single-storey structure 14.9 metres by 10.1 metres, with a double-gabled roof. Converted in 1768 into a Quaker meeting house with two rooms (including a meeting room in the northern half of the structure),

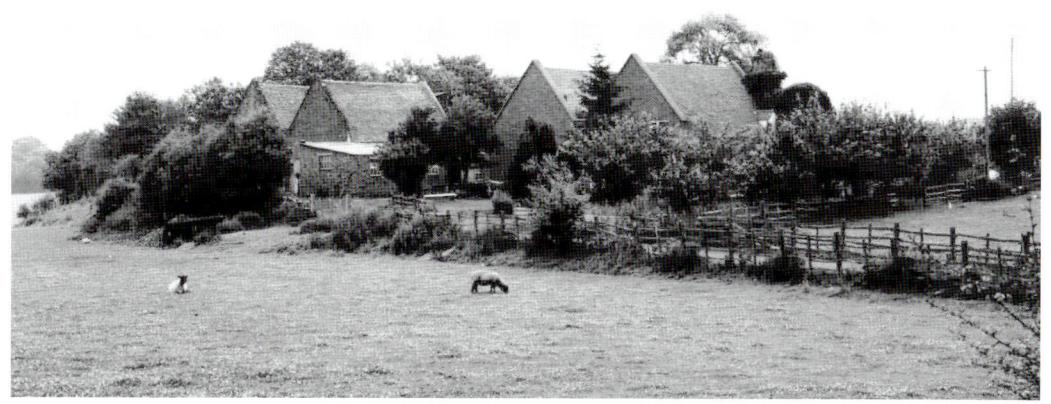

The surviving 1760s furnace buildings, later converted into a Quaker meeting house, at Newdale during the 1980s, shortly before demolition. (© Ironbridge Gorge Museum Trust)

the original building had a single floor area, with a row of columns supporting the valley between the two roofs. Excavation of the floor revealed the base of two brick pillars and a large square, brick-lined casting pit 3 metres by 3 metres in plan in the south-west corner. This still contained black casting sand and the impression of the final casting in the pit, a cylindrical object 6 feet (0.6 metres) long and 60 inches (1.52 metres) to 90 inches (2.29 metres) wide. The South Building was almost identical in construction and plan form. It was later converted and expanded into a farmhouse and barn. Excavation of the interior floor revealed a double row of post holes from an earlier structure. This was replaced by further iron working features from the 1760s, including a small irregularly shaped casting pit just 0.3 metres deep in the north-western corner of the building. At the southern end of the structure was a rectangular brick-lined pit, perhaps for holding water.

The 1987 excavation of one of the furnace buildings at Newdale by Ironbridge archaeologists. (© Ironbridge Gorge Museum Trust)

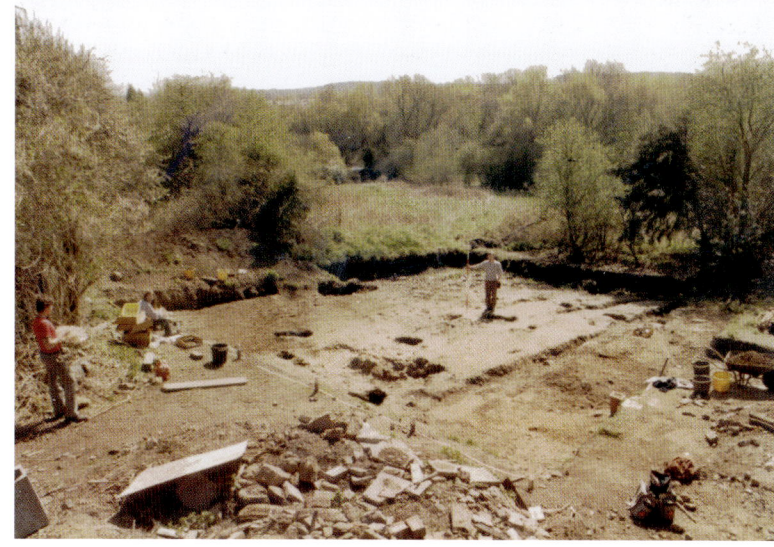

Between these buildings were two small brick-built furnaces, T-shaped in plan, whilst two roughly circular areas of slag to the east suggested the location of further furnaces. Beyond the buildings to the east were the badly damaged brick foundations of a fifth furnace, perhaps a cupola furnace.

The three sets of 1760s workers' housing were demolished in the 1960s. However, extensive excavation revealed the foundations of the houses forming Long Row and North Row, as well as the school building. No remains survived of a third set of workers' housing, West Row. North Row began life as an open-sided brick structure before being converted into three two-storey cottages in the early nineteenth century. Additional rooms and a wash house were added to the range in the 1900s and 1910s. Long Row lay *c.* 150 metres south-east of the rest of the complex and was a two-storey row of brick-built back-to-back houses, 61 metres long and 7.3 metres wide, a dividing spine wall giving eighteen two room houses in total. Photographs show they had a double-gabled tiled roof. Built before 1794 and probably before 1770, these are amongst the oldest back-to-back houses to be excavated in Britain.

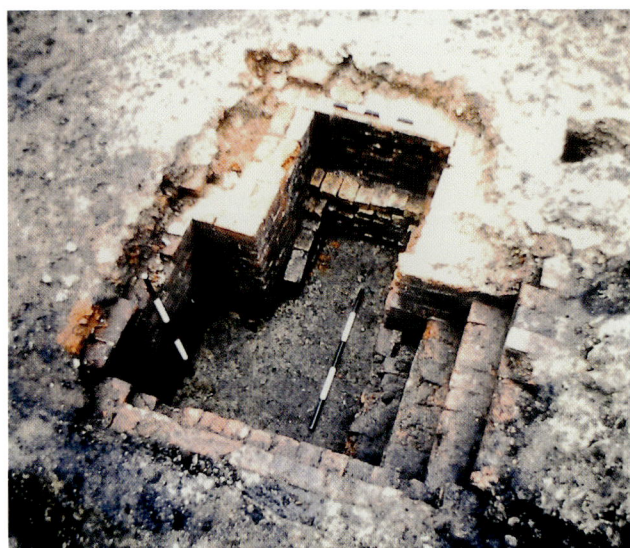

Left: One of the small brick-built furnaces, T-shaped in plan, found between the two former furnace buildings. (© Ironbridge Gorge Museum Trust)

Below: An early twentieth-century view of the Long Row back-to-back workers' housing at Newdale. (© Ironbridge Gorge Museum Trust)

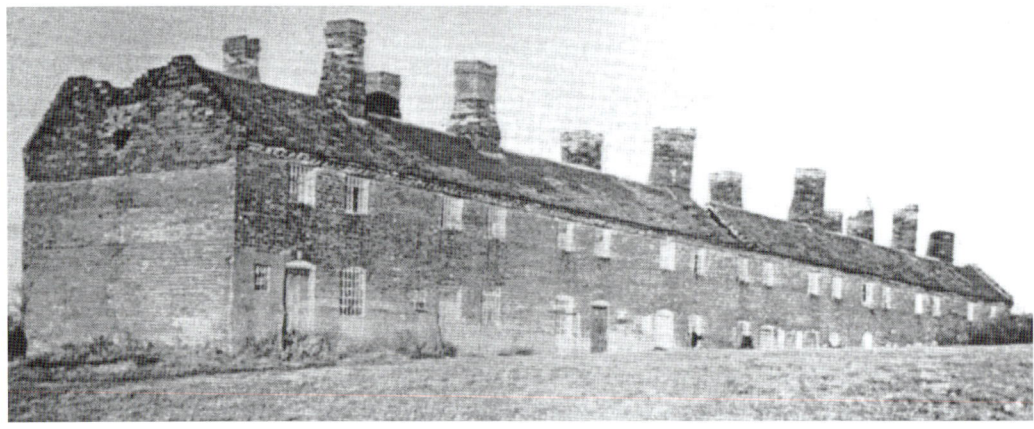

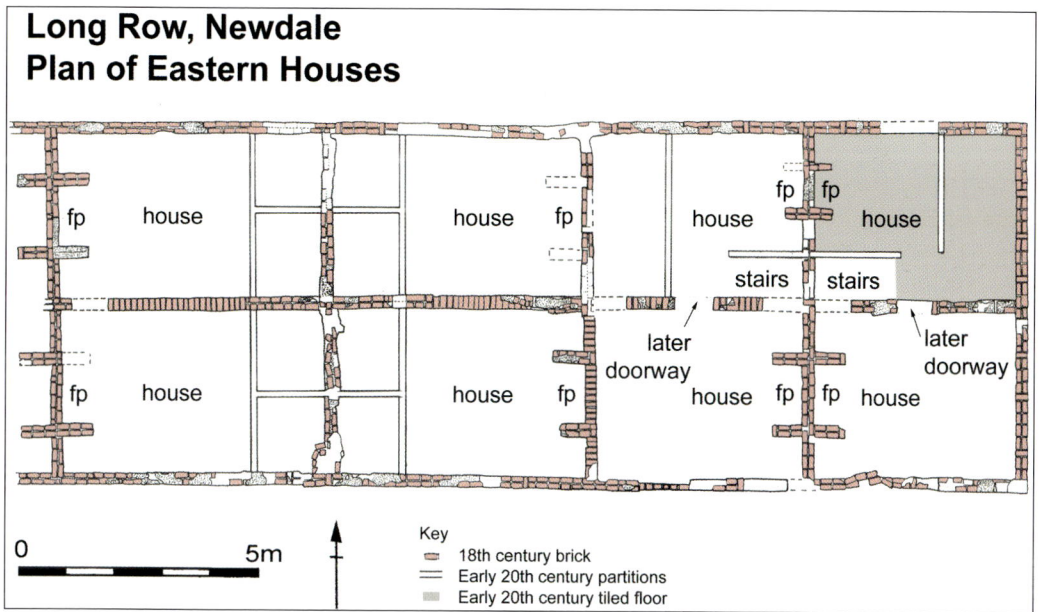

Long Row, Newdale
Plan of Eastern Houses

Key
- 18th century brick
- Early 20th century partitions
- Early 20th century tiled floor

0   5m

Excavated plan of the 1760s Long Row workers' housing as uncovered by Ironbridge archaeologists in 1987. This was one of the first industrial workers' housing excavations in Britain.

According to its business records, the Coalbrookdale Company first cast-iron rails in 1767. These were designed to be fixed to the top of a wooden track. However, it was not until the excavations at Newdale in 1987 that physical evidence for these first iron rails were located. Surprisingly, three sections of iron rail were found not on the railway alignment but reused as a lintel within a fireplace in the North Building of the ironworks, which was converted into a Quaker meeting house in 1768. These sections of iron rail had holes for bolts at either end and closely matched later historical illustrations. They are thus the earliest such iron rails found in the area (Clark & Alfrey, 1993, 71).

The excavation and survey work at Newdale was pioneering in three ways. This was the first time in the Gorge that a complete industrial settlement had been studied by combining excavation and survey work. Furthermore, the excavation of the back-to-back housing at Long Row was an early example of the archaeological study of this typical domestic building type of the new industrial age. Finally, archaeological excavation allowed the study of the iron working manufacturing processes in detail, an approach that would become normal practice in the 1990s and 2000s within the Gorge, and beyond.

Dig 11

Broseley Pipeworks Excavation and Survey (1987–93)

The process buildings and bottle-shaped kilns that make up the Broseley Pipeworks site lie south of the River Severn in Broseley, on the eastern side of King Street. The clay tobacco pipe was introduced in the seventeenth century, and its shape and maker's stamp makes it a key datable artefact on post-medieval and industrial sites. The factory stands at the southern end of Broseley Wood, an area that developed separately from the town of Broseley after enclosure from the common, as a small-scale industrial settlement from

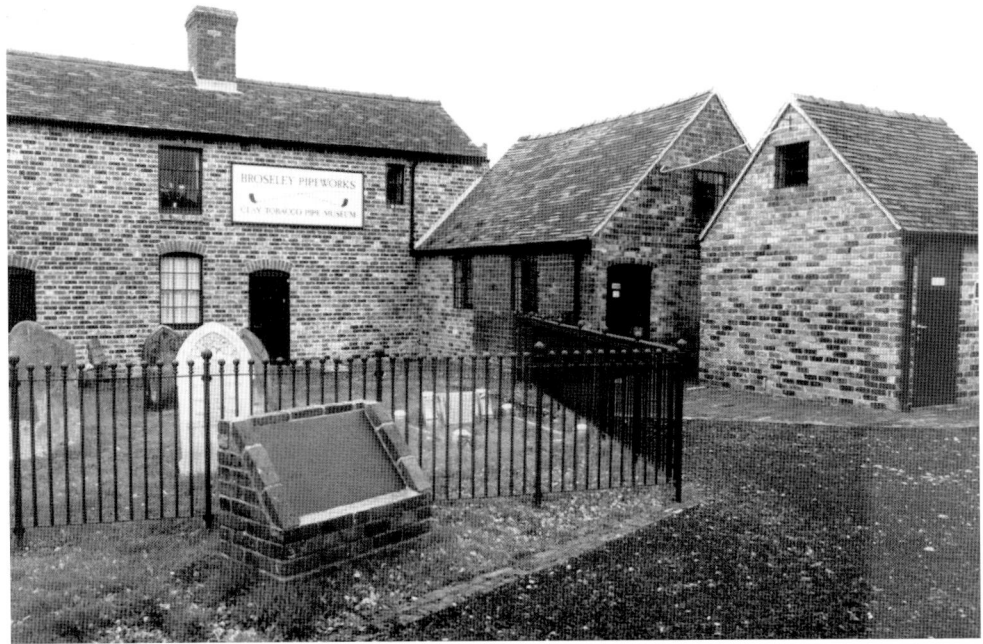

The main elevation of the nineteenth-century Broseley Pipeworks. (© Ironbridge Gorge Museum Trust)

the late seventeenth century onwards. Clay tobacco pipe manufacture in Broseley, which used the local white-firing clays and locally dug coal, began in the 1630s, with Broseley Wood and Benthall becoming the focus of small-scale workshops in the eighteenth century. During the nineteenth century this industry became concentrated into three firms, William Southorn & Co., Edwin Southorn, and Rowland Smitherman & Co., although clay tobacco pipe manufacturing remained a hand rather than a mechanised production process (Trinder, 2016, 113–114).

The Broseley clay tobacco pipeworks was established as the Crown Pipeworks on King Street in 1881 by Rowland Smitherman. The buildings were converted from earlier industrial structures, principally a cotton manufactory dating from the late eighteenth century, although in 1802 this site included a malthouse situated at the cotton factory and was operated by Lister and Blaise. The tobacco pipeworks business passed to Smitherman's son, also Rowland, on his death in 1903, but in 1923 was sold to William Southorn & Co., although there was a break in production until the 1930s. When manufacturing began once more, the site was making a variety of products including slip-cast pottery, only reverting to clay tobacco pipes in the 1950s. The works closed shortly afterwards in 1960 (Clark, 1993, 52–54).

During the complex's conversion into a museum in the mid-1980s, initial archaeological recording was undertaken (1987–88). This coincided with extensive archaeological

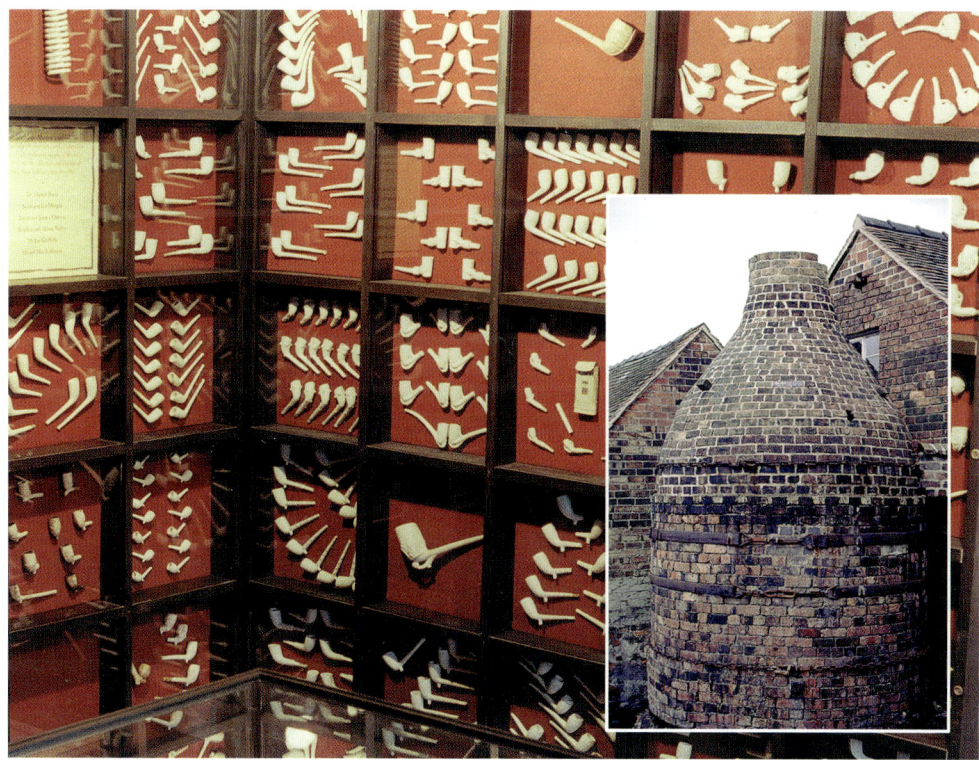

The surviving kiln at the Broseley Pipeworks with some of the clay tobacco pipe designs on display. Manufacture of such pipes was introduced in the Gorge in the Broseley area during the seventeenth century. (© Ironbridge Gorge Museum Trust)

research on the wider Broseley tobacco pipe manufacturing industry (Higgins, 1987). The initial survey work was followed in 1992–93 by detailed recorded work of the Broseley Pipeworks' buildings. This work recorded in detail the brick-built two-storey North Range and three-storey West Range (which fronted King Street), the two-storey East Range (built as a pair of cottages), and a circular bottle kiln with a detached chimney stack. These structures were all set around a courtyard. In addition, a single-storey schoolroom lay east of the kiln, whilst a Quaker burial ground lay in the angle between the school room and East Range (Higgins, Morriss & Trueman, 1988).

The archaeological survey work revealed that the North, West, and East Ranges were adapted and enlarged from earlier structures. The North Range was the earliest building and was probably originally a stable with a loft. The northern end of this range was added soon after as an agricultural barn. The West Range was converted into four cottages in the early nineteenth century. The two cottages that formed the East Range were added in the mid-nineteenth century. The adaptation of these buildings as a factory in the 1880s involved converting the rooms on the second and third floor of the West Range into workshops for moulding and preparation of the clay pipes. The lower storey of the East Range was also used as a preparation area, while packing was probably done of the ground floor of either the North or West Range. A first-floor walkway linked these ranges. The kiln was built in 1881 but the original chimney was replaced in the early twentieth century (Horton, 1997).

Having been bought by Bridgnorth District Council, it was decided to convert the site into a museum to be run by IGMT. The Broseley Pipeworks is now the only surviving clay tobacco pipe manufactory in Britain where the contents of the factory remain intact, but also where clay pipes continue to be made.

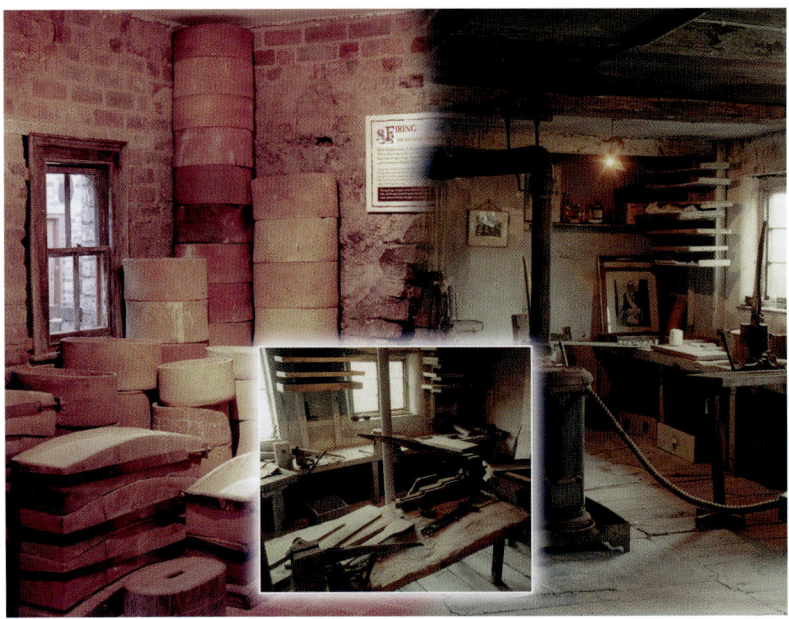

Clay tobacco pipe workshops with their original machinery at the Broseley Pipeworks. (© Ironbridge Gorge Museum Trust).

Dig 12

Madeley Wood Brick and Tile Works (1988–97)

On the eastern bank of the Shropshire Canal at Blists Hill stands the extensive remains of the Madeley Wood Company's brick and tile works. The site spans both banks of the canal, the earliest, and most complete, element being the eastern works where the surviving brick and tile process buildings cover 1.2 hectares. These buildings, which include four drying sheds, three kilns, two preparation sheds, and an engine house with two boilers and two chimneys, date mostly from the 1870s and 1880s and form a brick and tile works complex typical for the period. A late nineteenth-century extension to the works sits on the western side of the canal and was connected to the east works by an aerial incline across the canal.

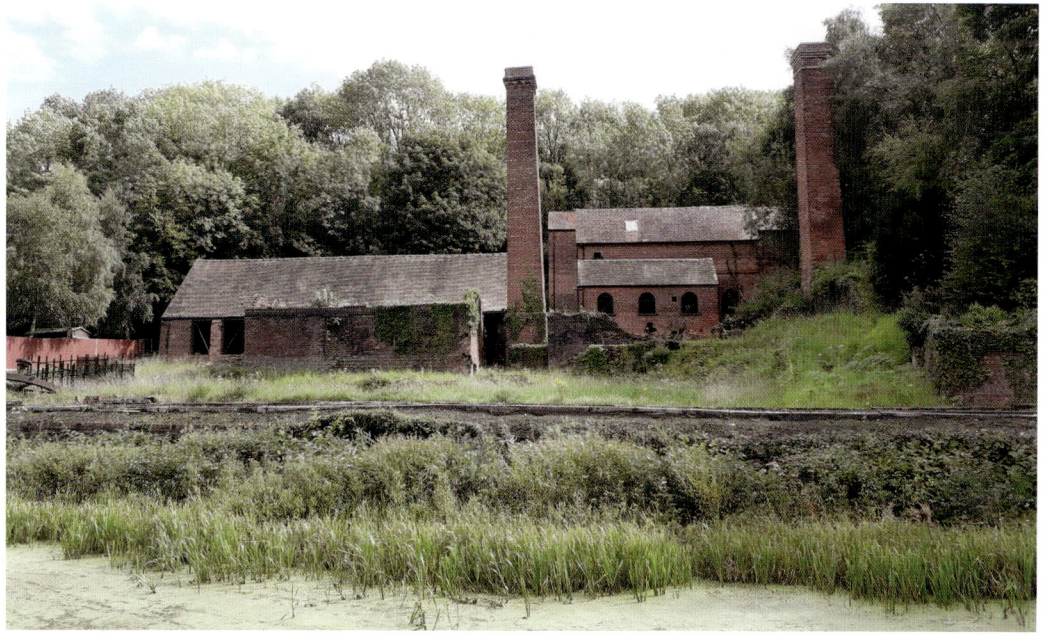

The late nineteenth-century Madeley Wood Brick and Tile Works buildings on the eastern side of the Shropshire Canal in 2020.

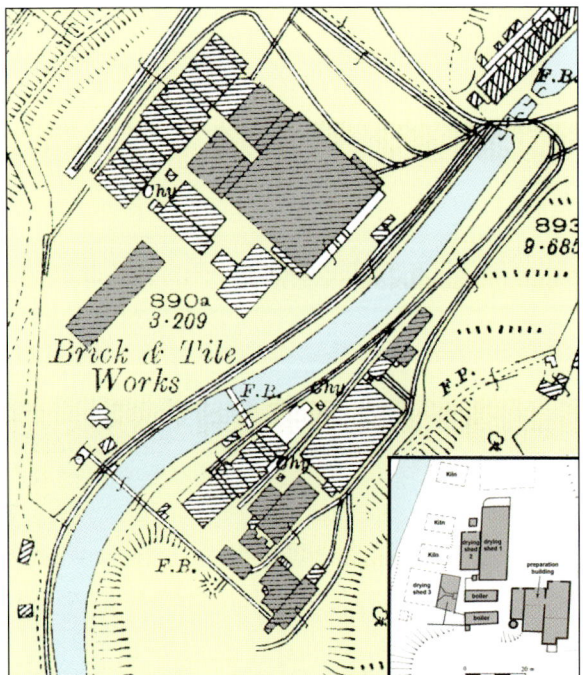

The Madeley Wood Brick and Tile Works as shown on a 1900s Ordnance Survey map of the area. By this date the works straddled both the western and eastern sides of the Shropshire Canal, with the buildings linked by wagonway and an overhead incline. The buildings of the eastern works are shown in the inset.

Brick and tile production was once very common within the Gorge, exploiting the area's clays and complimenting the pottery industry (Dig 11). Brick and tile production in Ironbridge boomed during the nineteenth century with forty-five extraction and production sites known: nineteen north of the river in Dawley and Madeley, and twenty-six sites south of the river in Benthall and Broseley. The buildings at most of these sites, apart from Jackfield (Dig 7) and the Maw & Co.'s Benthall works, have long since vanished, so the survival of a near intact works at Blists Hill is an important reminder of how extensive the industry once was.

The Madeley Wood Company first built a small brickworks with one kiln on the eastern side of the canal at Blists Hills by 1847, extracting clay from adjacent pits. This was rebuilt in the period 1872 to 1883 with the addition of a new kiln and two new drying sheds. This was a period of innovation within the industry. Increased mechanisation saw clay preparation machinery introduced run by steam engines, replacing more traditional hand production, and drying sheds heated with the waste heat. Even the kiln designs were improved using the more efficient down-draught types. The Madeley Wood Company was also the owners of the Blists Hill Mine (Dig 9) west of the canal and from 1879 it supplied both coal and clay to the enlarged brickworks (Clark, 1993, 69). Large scale expansion occurred in the years 1883 to 1902 when the clay preparation block was extended, a second boiler was added to the power plant and a new works office built. The focus of this expansion, however, was west of the canal, where new drying sheds and kilns were built on what had been the coke yard for the blast furnaces at Blists Hill, then in decline. An advert for the company in 1900 boasted of production 'made by the most modern process or hand-made', with products including 'plain and ornamental ridge tiles, finials, hip, valley and angle tiles, best white facing bricks, plinths etc, fire bricks, burrs and squares and all kinds of brick-kiln goods'.

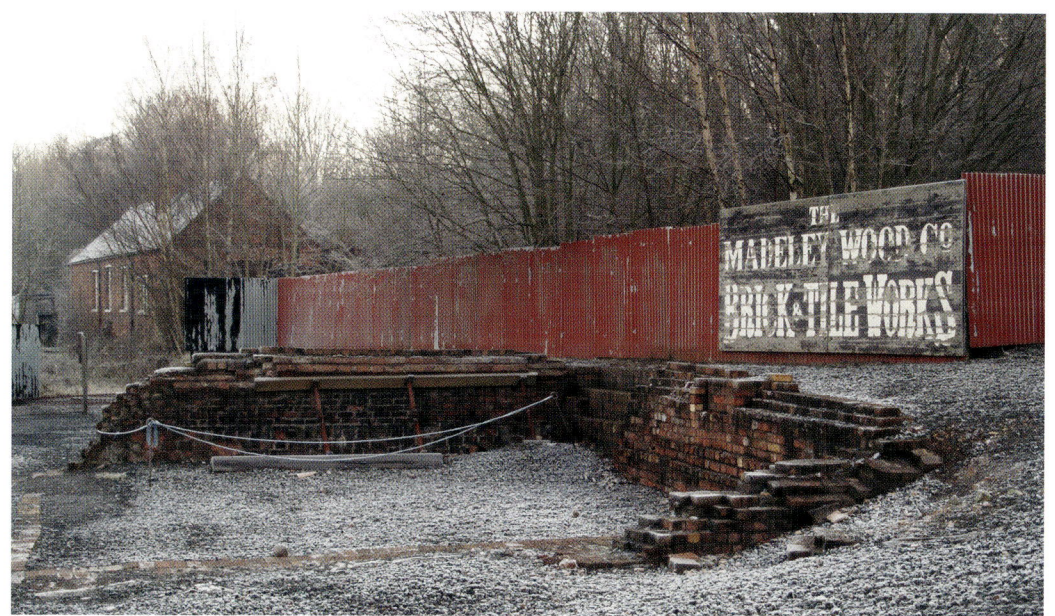

Above: One of the 1870s drying kilns at the Madeley Wood works, excavated in the 1990s by Ironbridge archaeologists.

Right: The 1870s drying sheds at the Madeley Wood works in 2020.

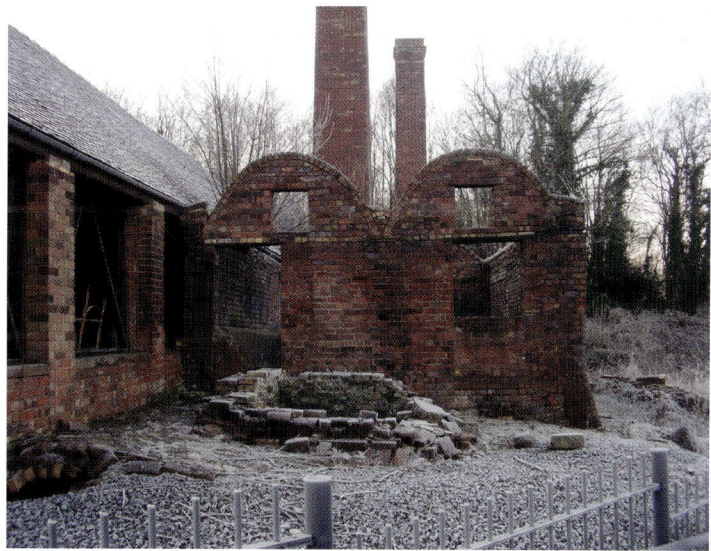

   In 1912 the site was leased by George Legge & Sons, who bought the complex in 1916. Although the new owner built an aerial inclined plane to link the two production sites by 1925, activity at the east works declined in favour of the larger west works, the kilns being abandoned by the mid-1920s. Clay preparation became the main focus of its activities, which might be why drying shed No. 2 was converted into a water tank and the aerial incline built. Oral history recordings suggest that the east works also concentrated on handmade tiles, moulded in hand-operated presses, in the remaining drying sheds. Machine-made bricks were produced at the west works (Hayman, Horton & White, 1999, 104–106).

George Legge & Sons closed in 1938 and after a period of abandonment in 1945 the firm of John Raleigh, who also operated the Benthall Pipeworks south of the river, began making sanitary pipes using the larger western works, finally closing in 1956 (Hayman, Horton & White, 1999, 106). It seems likely that the eastern works was not reused.

After the closure of the brick and tile works, the Blists Hill site lay mostly abandoned until the late 1960s. As late as the mid-1960s parts of the tile works were being lost, the chimney to the western brick drying sheds being demolished in this period. However, the growing interest in conserving the industrial past of the Gorge at the Old Furnace from the late 1950s and the development of Telford new town from the mid-1960s led to the establishment of the Ironbridge Gorge Museum Trust in 1967 and Blists Hill was chosen as the site for a new open-air museum, the tile works being one of the key sites. The new museum would also reflect the social history of the area, rescuing Victorian buildings at risk form the development of Telford new town. Some of these were re-erected at Blists Hill. After several buildings had been reconstructed on the site, Blists Hill Open Air Museum opened in 1973, and the late nineteenth-century single-storey brick drying sheds to the west of the canal were converted into museum warehouses and workshops for the new visitor attraction.

Initial conservation work on the brick and tile works complex east of the canal was not undertaken until 1988, and full archaeological recording did not take place until the 1990s. These included boiler settings, a clay preparation block and the engine house with its tall chimney stack, four drying sheds (the large drying shed No. 1 with a pitched and tiled roof; drying shed No. 2 with an unusual two-span barrel-vaulted roof; the foundations of drying shed No. 3; and the site of drying shed No. 4), and the site of the three drying kilns. The latter were excavated in 1988. The clay preparation block, its engine house and boiler bases, were recorded and planned in 1994–95. In 1998 the standing remains of drying shed No. 1 and drying shed No. 2 were also recorded. Small-scale excavation in 1995 revealed a pair of parallel flues linking the northern kiln with drying shed No. 2, whilst in 1998 the northern end of the drying shed was cleared and excavated.

The importance of the brick and tile works buildings at Blists Hill lies both in their completeness and the tight date for their construction, with most built during the period 1872 to 1883 at a time when new production processes were being introduced. They thus capture the dynamism of an industry innovating to meet the expanding communities of the late nineteenth century.

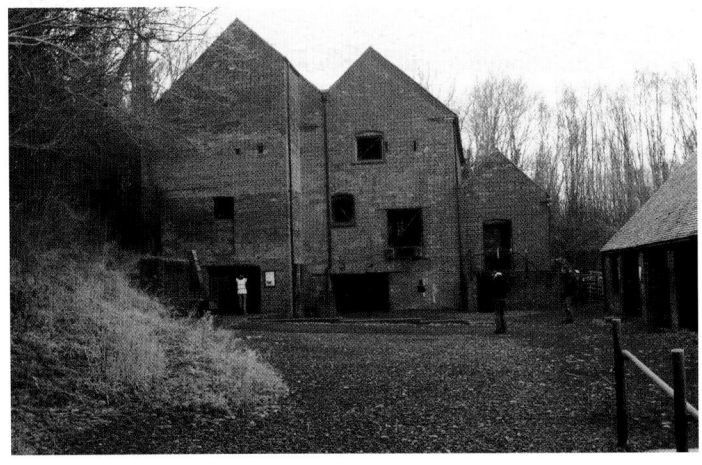

The 1870s preparation shed at the Madeley Wood works in 2020.

Dig 13

The Coalport Canal (1992–2003)

The restoration of the abandoned Coalport terminus of the Shropshire Canal began in the mid-1970s when the Coalport China Works was being converted into one of the new museum sites for the Ironbridge Gorge Museum Trust (Dig 6). This isolated stretch of the Shropshire Canal, known locally as the Coalport Canal, played an import part in opening the eastern end of the Gorge to industry at the end of the eighteenth century.

In 1780 a wooden bridge was built across the river at Preens Eddy. In 1818 it was replaced by a cast-iron bridge (Dig 17), whilst wharves, quays, and warehouses sprang up around the new crossing. However, it was the construction of the Shropshire

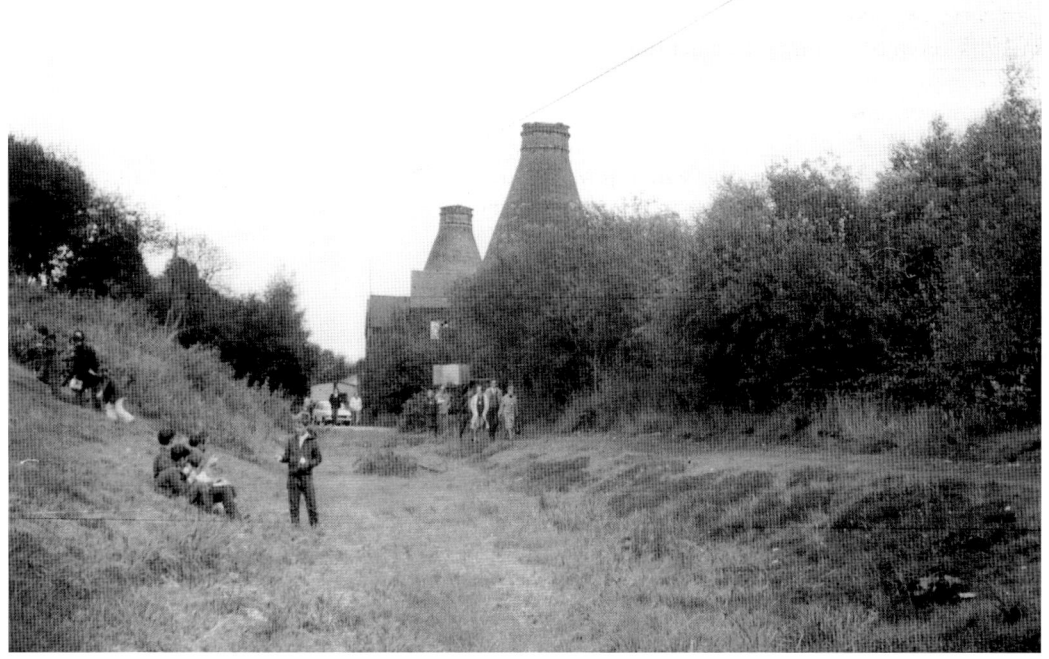

The abandoned Coalport Canal running to the north of the surviving kilns of the China Works as photographed in the early 1970s. (© Ironbridge Gorge Museum Trust)

Canal that boosted industry at the eastern end of the Gorge. The 17.7 km route of the canal had been surveyed by William Reynolds in 1787, the aim being to link the East Shropshire Coalfield with the River Severn. The first section was started in 1788 and went from Wrockwardine Wood and the junction with the earlier Donnington Wood Canal, southwards to Southall Bank, where a branch ran westwards to Coalbrookdale. The main stretch continued southwards using an incline plane at Windmill to drop 38.4 metres, then ran through Blists Hill before reaching the top of The Hay, from where it dropped via another incline plain a further 63 metres, over 320 metres, to Coalport. A 90 degree turn to the east brought canal parallel to, but above, the River Severn. 1,200m later it ended just to the west of the Wooden Bridge (Hadfield, 1966, 153–154; Trinder, 2016, 106–107; Trinder 2000, 88).

The Shropshire Canal Company granted permission for William Reynolds to pile the canal banks to allow for wharves and other developments along the canal and river. At the eastern terminus of the canal, Reynolds built a large warehouse straddling the waterway and stretching to the riverbank, and a stop lock was also planned to link the canal with the river (Hadfield, 1966, 157). Such a lock would have been difficult to operate due to the floodwaters of the Severn and the tendency of this area to subsidence. It was also too small to take the large trows which sailed up and down the River Severn, rather than the smaller tub boats used on the canal. This is probably why self-acting inclines were used to transfer goods between the river and the canal at this point (Horton, Richardson, Sherratt, White & Worthington, 1993). By 1794 the canal interchange, wharves, and industries at the foot of the Hay Inclined Plane were being referred to as Coalport.

In the early years of the canal, road transport was still heavily relied upon and a number of new roads were put through the area. The road from Worcester to Wellington, which used the Preens Eddy Bridge, was completed in 1797. Other roads, such as that from Preens Eddy Bridge through to Ironbridge, were constructed by the bridge proprietors (Clark & Alfrey, 1986, 81).

New business began to appear within a few years of the canal opening. A Hemp Ropeworks was in operation in 1794, and the chainworks of William Horton was established in 1798. A timber works appeared sometime after 1800, along with a bag-making factory (Clark & Alfrey, 1986, 83–84). By 1803 around thirty cottages had been built in this area and by 1807 one group had been leased to John Rose for his china works (Dig 6). Reynolds also shared with Thomas Bryan of the Tuckies estate the ownership of the ferry that daily brought the workers from Jackfield to Coalport (Trinder, 2000, 88). Although Coalport established itself as a new commercial centre, it remained in the shadow of nearby Madeley, which continued to be the commercial and social focus of the area, north of the river, with its own market and church.

Excavation and survey work had already begun on part of the Shropshire Canal in 1969–70 with the exploration of the Hay Inclined Plane and the adjacent part of the Shropshire Canal. As noted in Dig 3, this inclined plane railway linked the upper stretch of the Shropshire Canal with the lower Coalport Canal. The basin at the foot of the incline and its associated sandstone-built loading bay, where the tub boats transferred to the inclined plane, were cleared and repaired in 1974 (Hayman, Horton & White, 1999, 125). To the east, part of the isolated stretch of canal between the incline and the Coalport China Museum was also restored in 1974 but using wooden planks and iron tie bars for the canal sides.

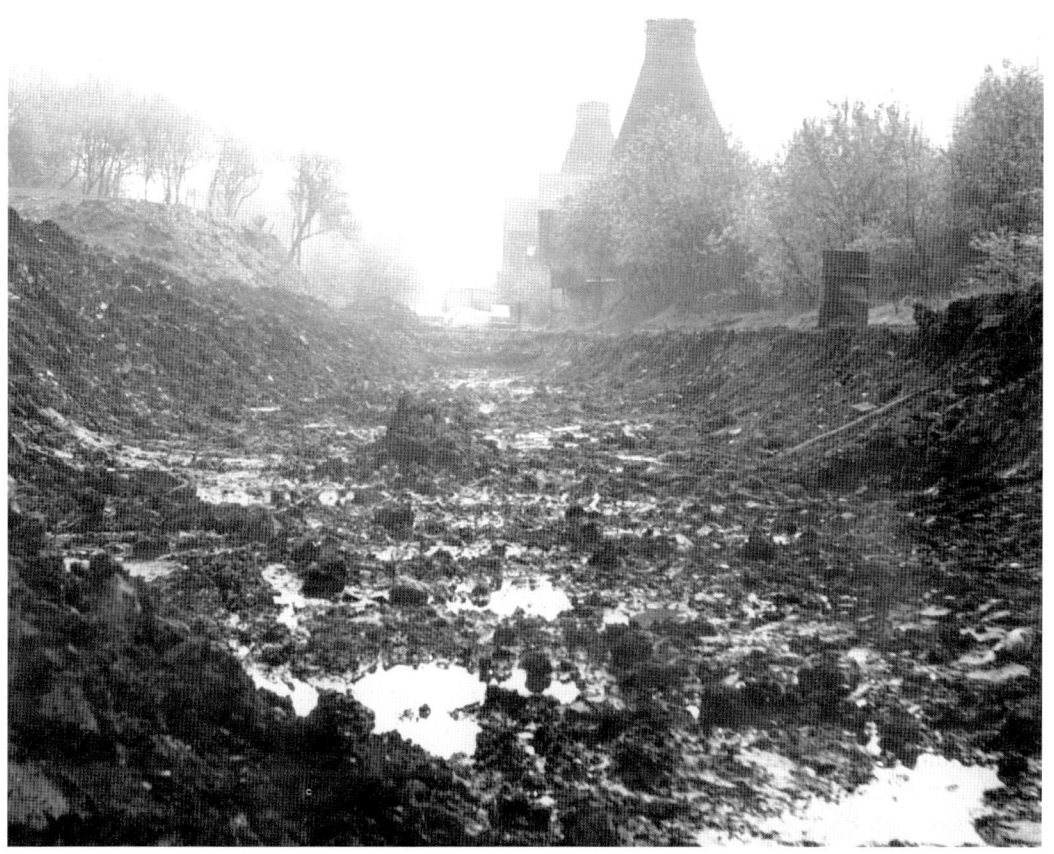

The excavation in 1974 of the Coalport Canal looking east towards the Coalport China Works. (© Ironbridge Gorge Museum Trust)

There was no serious attempt to record this stretch of the canal archaeologically until 1992. This work was undertaken as part of the Severn Gorge Repairs project with the aim of restoring the collapsing walls of the Blists Hill and Coalport stretches of canal, replacing the wooden walls at Coalport, and sealing leaks along the two lengths due to subsidence (Horton, Richardson, Sherratt, White & Worthington, 1993). Restoration work within the basin at the foot of the inclined plane revealed a timber beam, held in place by iron tie bars, that ran along the east and west facing walls. This would have acted as a buffer to protect the masonry when the tub boats bumped against the side of the basin. The work also recorded the vertical grooves for a stop lock at the southern end of the basin. Fifteen test pits around the canal basin and along a 180-metre stretch of the canal through the China Works recorded the fragmentary brick and sandstone fabric of the canal's walls. A feature of the upper layers of those test pits, along the southern edge of the canal, was evidence for the dumping of kiln waste such as ash, pottery, porcelain, kiln furniture, and slag (Horton, Richardson, Sherratt, White & Worthington, 1993).

In 2003 another opportunity arose to explore the wharves along the canal. In that year excavation work was undertaken by Ironbridge Archaeology to the north and at the eastern end of the Coalport China Museum (IGMT, 2003). Three trenches were dug, one of which focussed on the canal structure. This trench (Trench 3) located the most complete surviving section of canal walls, showing it was originally 2 metres deep. Trench 1 on the northern side of the museum, indicated that the area had been used for dumping ash from the kilns but there was no sign of any pottery waste from ceramic factories, as had been seen in 1992.

The main route of the Shropshire Canal closed in 1857, after being leased to the London & North Western Railway in 1854. However, the section between Blists Hill and Coalport remained in use until at least 1902, the Coalport Canal finally being abandoned and backfilled in 1920. The railway was closed in 1963 (Clark & Alfrey, 1986, 75–76). With the restoration of the Coalport branch of the canal in the 1970s and 1980s, it is once more possible to appreciate the landscape importance of the waterway in boosting the industrial development of this part of the Gorge.

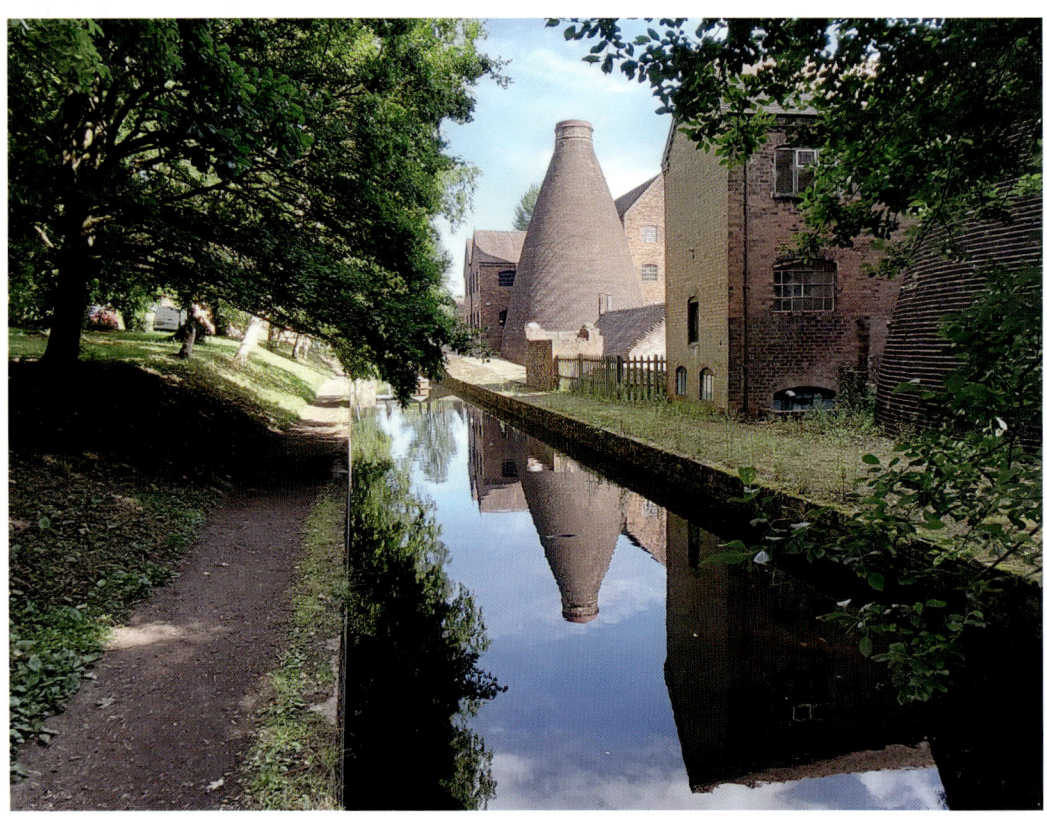

The same view of the Coalport Canal looking east towards the Coalport China Works in 2022.

Dig 14

The Lloyds Engine House (1996)

Lying within Lloyds Coppice, on the north side of the River Severn, foundations of the Lloyds Engine House can be found the stone. This part of Madeley Wood lies 1.5 kilometres east of Ironbridge and 0.5 kilometres west of Blists Hill. It is a steeply sloping area where several seams of coal, fireclay, ironstone, and sandstone outcrop are found, and as a result the area saw intensive mining activity from the early eighteenth to the early twentieth centuries (Brown, 1991, 5–6; Trinder, 2016, 108).

The first steam engine to pump water out of a mine in the Ironbridge area was erected at Madeley in 1719. A reference from 1726 mentions 'Smiths Gin Pit situate and being in the Lloyds', which might suggest that this 1719 engine is the one at Lloyds. However, a later reference from 1745 mentions a 'new engine in Madeley Wood' so the original date of the engine is unclear. Ownership of the mine passed to Richard Reynolds, manager at the Coalbrookdale Company, who bought the manor of Madeley in 1781–82. The site, along with several other mines including that at Blists Hill, was run by the Reynolds and later the Anstice families before being abandoned in 1913 (Hayman, 1997, 39, 48; Baggs, Cox, McFall, Stamper & Winchester, 1985, 46–47).

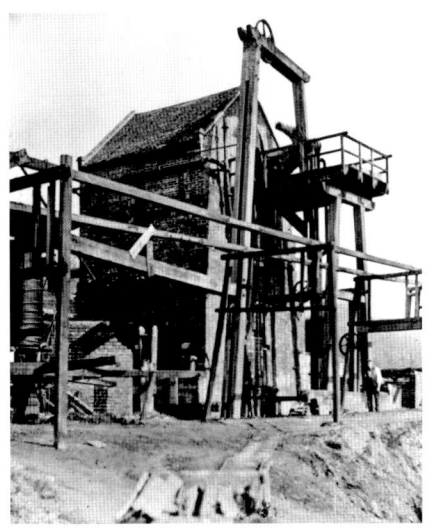

A 1912 view of the Lloyds mine pumping engine at the time of its initial abandonment. (© Ironbridge Gorge Museum Trust)

A brief three-day excavation in 1970 by local volunteer archaeologists demonstrated the extensive survival of the stone and brick foundations of the engine house. Within the adjacent pumping shaft the pump rod from the last engine was located, although this had to be truncated due to safety fears in the 1980s (Hayman 1997, 38–39). Excavation by Ironbridge archaeologists in 1996 revealed the near square-plan brick foundations of the engine house, 6.3 metres by 6 metres. Inside was an engine bed of handmade bricks on which the cylinder sat, with two phases of brickwork visible. Two of the original four iron fixing bolts, used to hold down the cylinder, were found to still be in place. Immediately to the south was the 3.5-metres-deep condenser pit. The thicker southern wall marked the location of the 'bob' wall on which the beam pivoted. The beam projected beyond the southern wall of the engine house over the oval pumping shaft, 3.2 metres at its widest, which was lined with machine-made bricks. At the bottom of the pumping shaft were large sections of timber and ironwork.

A description of the engine survives from 1912 in an American magazine called *Power*, which notes that the open-topped cylinder was 26 inches (0.66 metres) in diameter, with an 8-foot stroke and that the cast-iron beam was 20 feet (6.1 metres) long. Two pumps, each of 9.75 inch (0.25 metre) bore, were used to lift water from the mine 91 metres below in 45-metre stretches. Photographs show the engine house standing roughly 10 metres in height, with a pitched roof. The power for the engine was provided by two haystack boilers and a wagon boiler. This machinery was clearly not the fabric of the original engine and the writer noted that the equipment was around 115 years old, suggesting an installation date of *c*. 1800 (Brown, 1991, 11).

The earliest phase on the site was represented by the handmade brick engine house walls, with the two-phased engine bed added later. The pumping shaft must have been rebuilt much later since it was lined with machine-made brick. The archaeologists working in 1996 did not find any evidence to suggest this was the site of the engine mentioned in 1719, so it seems likely that this was the 'new engine' from 1745. Documentary evidence suggests that this mid-eighteenth-century Newcomen-type atmospheric engine was modified around 1800, as indicated by the two phases of engine bed and the addition of a separate condensing cylinder. It was altered again in

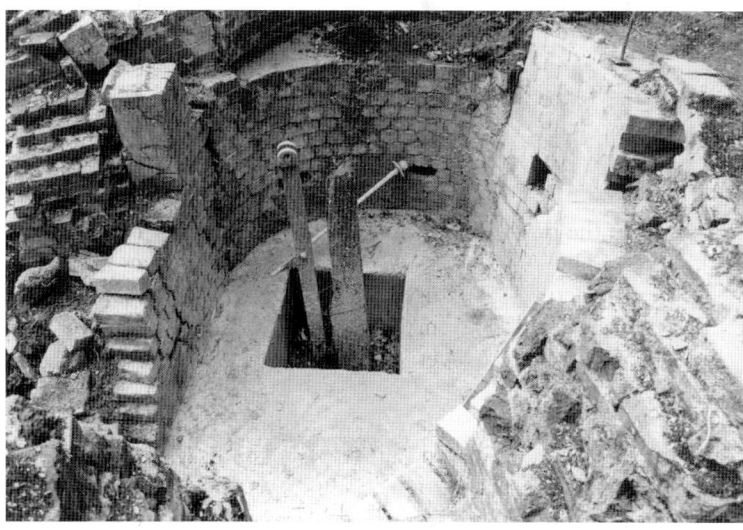

The top of the excavated and capped pumping shaft at Lloyds in 1996 showing the truncated pumping rod. (© Ironbridge Gorge Museum Trust)

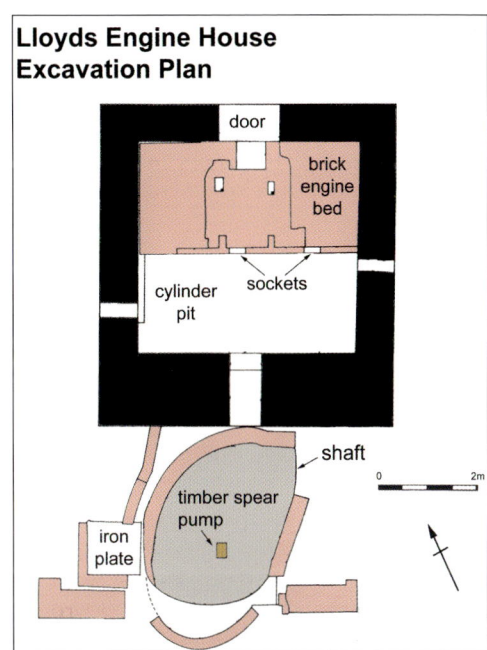

Excavation plan of the eighteenth- and nineteenth-century Lloyds Engine House, as revealed in 1996 by Ironbridge archaeologists.

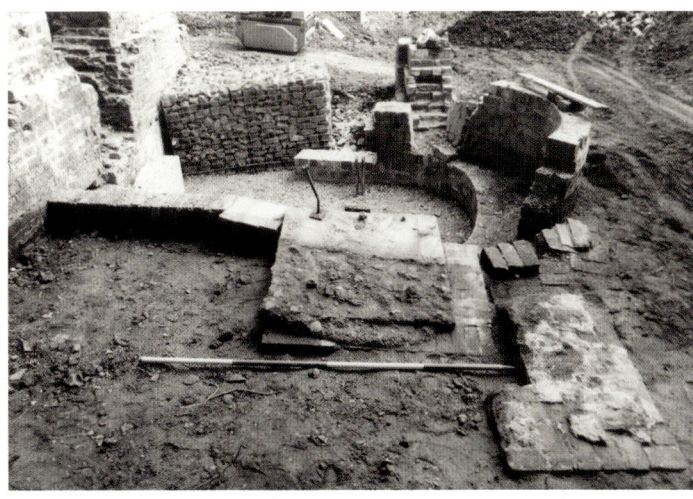

The 1996 excavations at Lloyds showing the top of the pumping shaft (centre) and the southern wall of the engine house (left). In the foreground is an engine bed with an iron plate covering. (© Ironbridge Gorge Museum Trust)

the later nineteenth century when the pumping shaft was rebuilt and a new boiler added (Hayman & Horton, 1999, 122). The 1996 work also recorded the lining of an earlier pool on the eastern side of these structures, later used to supply water to the boilers, and a small brick air shaft to the south-west of the engine house.

Historic maps and descriptions from the nineteenth century show that the Lloyds Engine House was part of much bigger mining landscape with several pits accessed by several railways, although these were not investigated in 1996. This engine house is the second eighteenth-century colliery pumping engine to be excavated in the Gorge, after that at Blists Hill Pit (Dig 9). The archaeological investigations in 1996 confirmed that this was the site of one of the earliest steam engines, not just in Ironbridge, but in Britain.

Dig 15

Upper Works Buildings, Coalbrookdale (2000–03)

The Upper Works, which includes Darby's 1709 furnace, is the most important of a series of forge and furnace sites that lie along the Dale Brook at the western end of the Gorge. These include not just the Upper Works, but the Lower Works, the Upper Forge (Dig 16), the Middle Forge, and the Lower Forge (Dig 19). The Upper Works was founded in the mid-seventeenth century and after Abraham Darby I took over the site and furnace in 1708, the complex expanded steadily down the valley during the eighteenth and nineteenth centuries to become one of the biggest ironworking concerns in the Gorge (Hayman, Horton & White, 1999, 14–15).

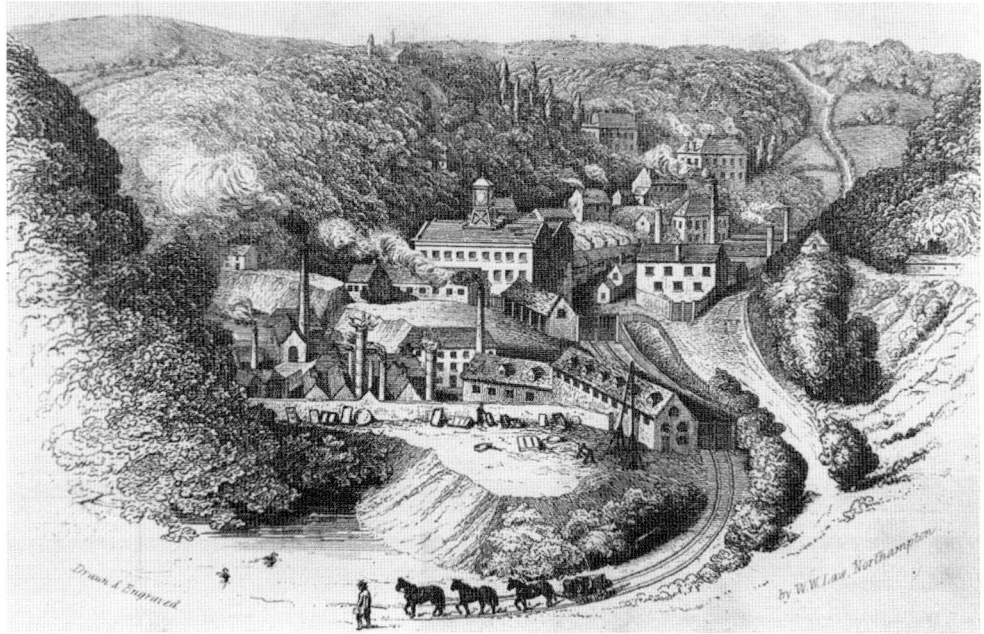

A *c.* 1843 engraving by W. W. Law looking north towards the Coalbrookdale Works. The clock tower of the Great Warehouse is now part of the Museum of Iron. This view also shows a wagonway running along Wellington Road south of the works. (© Ironbridge Gorge Museum Trust)

The works had an extensive range of process, production, and warehouse buildings, including furnaces, a turning mill, smithies, moulding workshops, engine shop, fitting workshops, carpenters' workshops, offices, and two furnace pools. A network of wagonways and later railways linked the ironworking complex to the north with the Shropshire Canal at Brierley Hill (see Dig 18) and to the south with The Wharfage along the northern bank of the River Severn (See Dig 8). Production at the Upper Works site started to decline after the site was taken over by Allied Ironfounders Ltd in 1922, who concentrated their production at the Lower Works. During the 1930s many of the buildings and railways south of the old furnace were cleared, the area close to the 1709 furnace being used for dumping foundry waste until the 1950s (Darby, 2010, 8).

Study of the Upper Works has been understandably dominated by archaeological and historical research on Darby's 1709 furnace and the pioneering role of this site in the use of coke to smelt iron (see Dig 1). There was some limited recording of the buildings south of this furnace in the 1980s. The Long Warehouse, a mid-nineteenth-century three-storey warehouse, sixteen bays long with ground floor workshops for grinding and dressing ranges and grates, was converted into an archive, library, and teaching building, and opened in 1983. The Great Warehouse, built in 1838 (the clock tower was added in 1843), was restored and opened as a museum in 1979, now the Museum

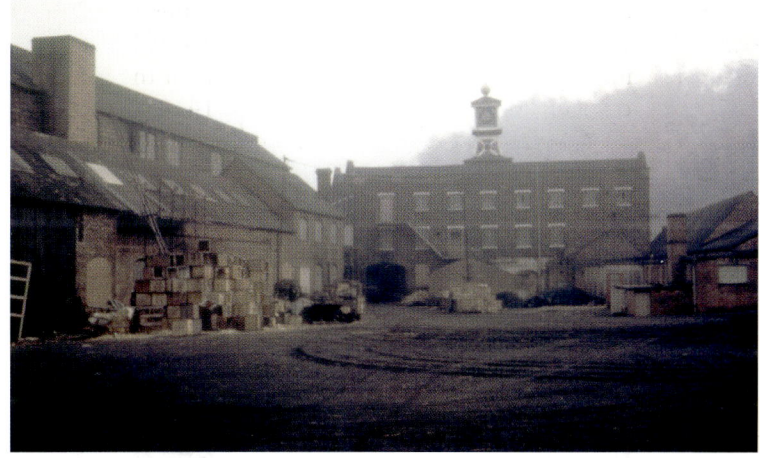

The Great Warehouse (centre) and Long Warehouse (left) as photographed by Kate Bishop in 1964 when the site was still being used by the Coalbrookdale Iron Company. (© Ironbridge Gorge Museum Trust)

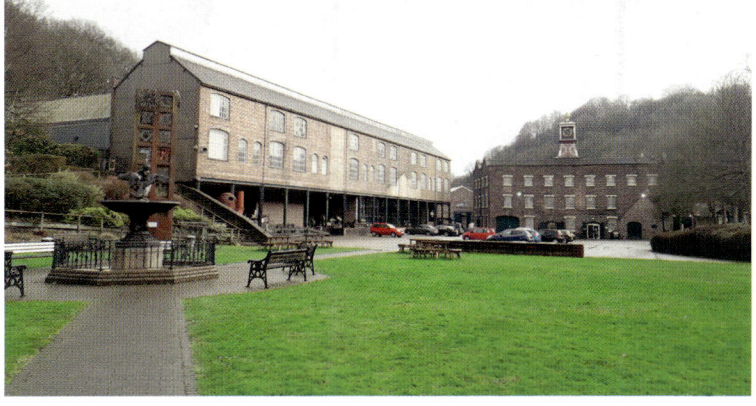

The same view in 2022 showing the restored Great Warehouse, now the Museum of Iron, and the Long Warehouse, now housing the IGMT archive and library.

of Iron (Trinder, 2017, 16). However, it was not until the early twenty-first century that archaeological research turned to the study of the rest of the southern buildings on the Upper Works site. Between 2000 and 2003, the Ironbridge Archaeology Unit undertook detailed recoding of these standing structures ahead of conservation work (Belford, 2009b and 2009c).

The Northern Lights structure, the former fitting shop to the east of, and abutting, the Long Warehouse, was built between 1883 and 1902. It was initially used as a fitting shop but by 1952 contained an enamelling shop and a dressing shop. The building was a single-storey structure built into the hillside and had cast-iron tiles and wooden blocks forming the flooring. The sawtooth or north light glazed roof had wooden king-post trusses supported by cast-iron columns, but there was also a mid-twentieth-century northern extension to the building, which had lightweight steel trusses. This latter part of the building was demolished, and excavation of the site revealed the rectangular brick base of a furnace. Close by a *c.* 5-metre length of iron railway was uncovered, which accessed some of the nineteenth-century buildings that preceded the building of the Northern Lights structure (Hayman & Horton, 1996).

The brick and stone office complex, which lies behind and to the south of the Great Warehouse, was used principally as the offices for the Coalbrookdale Company. It was

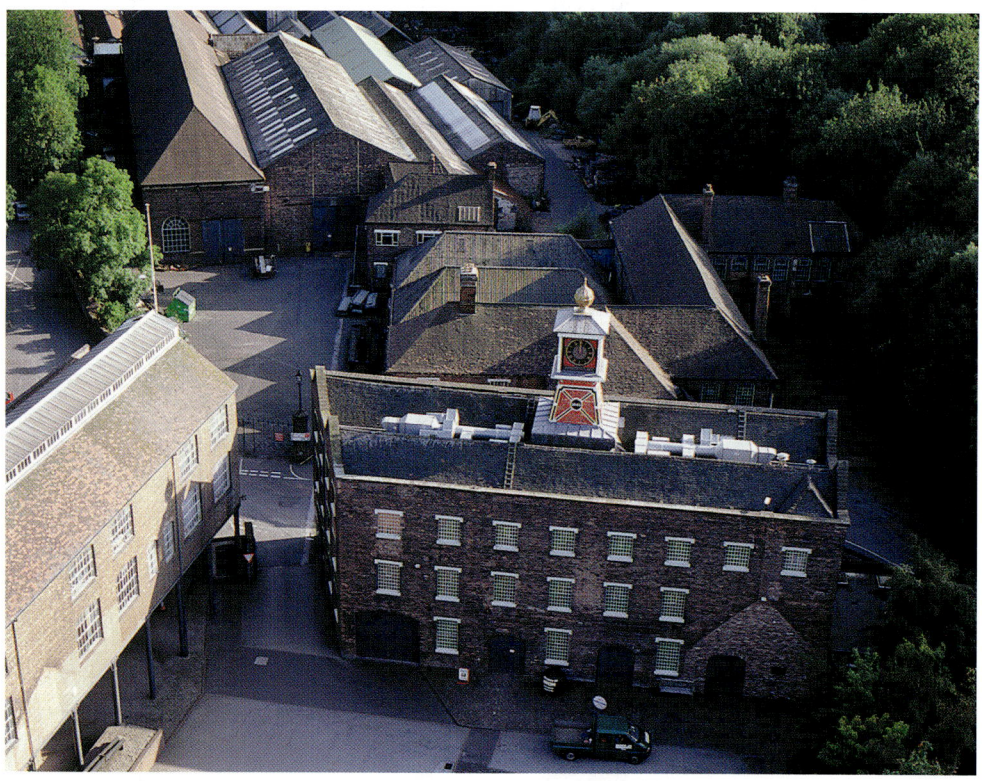

An aerial view from the early twenty-first century showing the Great Warehouse and its 1843 clock tower. Immediately behind this lie mid-nineteenth-century office buildings, and beyond these at the top of the photograph are the 1879–86 erecting shops, now home to 'Enginuity'. (© Ironbridge Gorge Museum Trust)

built in the period 1838–47 and extended in the later nineteenth century. Originally L-shaped in plan, it was lengthened and heightened to two storeys, with the addition of wings and canopied bays by 1883. The first-floor offices have cast-iron ceiling roses and ventilators, whilst the board room has a plaster cornice. The central range has cast-iron columns supporting the roof structure. To the east of the offices are a range of three single-storey open workshops, now the 'Enginuity' part of the museum. These were built in the mid-nineteenth century and had cast-iron columns supporting a timber roof. Excavation of the brick floors revealed a railway track bed in the southern bay (Hayman & White, 1995).

To the south of the offices lie the Erecting Shop and its associated buildings. This complex was sited over the Lower Furnace Pool, which was filled prior to these structures being built. It was a rectangular, single-storey building sixteen bays long, dominated by tall round-headed cast-iron windows, with railway access. The original eleven-bays were built in 1879 and expanded by the addition of a further five bays in 1883–86. The final phase of the complex was the rebuilding of the *c.* 1879 assembly shops around 1930. The interior was one large space with railway tracks giving access to the yard. The roof structure comprised timber tie-beam and collar trusses with steel struts. The western wall has fourteen blocked arches and high-level knuckle joints, which supported jib cranes and bearing boxes for a cable drive. Excavations at the southern end of the complex revealed the remains of a brick-lined cellar, 0.75 metres deep, *c.* 3 metres by 2 metres in plan.

Though less iconic than Darby's 1709 furnace, the surviving Upper Works buildings tell the later story of the Coalbrookdale Company and its ironwork. This research also shows how detailed archaeological recording can throw light on the complex development of the modest iron and engineering buildings of one of the earliest integrated ironworks in Britain.

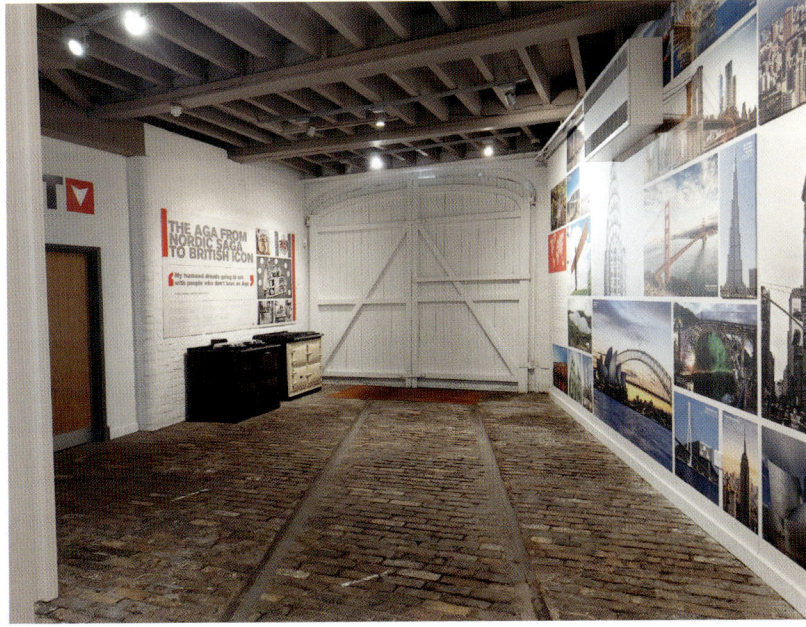

The interior of one of the bays of 1879–86 erecting shops showing surviving railway tracks used to move goods in and out of the buildings.

Dig 16

The Upper Forge Steel Works (2001–05)

The Upper Forge is one of the series of five forge and furnace sites that lie along the Dale Brook at the western end of the Gorge. These include the Upper Works, the Lower Works, the Upper Forge, the Middle Forge, and the Lower Forge (see Dig 1 and Dig 19). The Lower Forge and Middle Forge both date from the mid- to late sixteenth century, whilst the Upper Forge site appears to have been established right at the beginning of the seventeenth century (Belford, 2018, 137–144; Belford & Ross, 2007, 107; Clark, 1993, 43). The Lower Furnace and Upper Works (containing Darby's Old Furnace) appear to have been established slightly later in the mid-seventeenth century (Hayman, Horton & White, 1999, 36). There was thus a broadly chronological development of sites along the brook from south to north up the valley. In contrast by the early eighteenth century iron was smelted at the upper end of the dale, converted into wrought iron at the Upper Forge, part way down the valley, and worked into nails and frying pans at the bottom of the Dale by the river, in the Lower Furnace and Lower Forge.

In the twenty-first century only the Upper Forge buildings survive as above ground structures in the middle part of the Dale (Hayman, Horton & White, 1999, 39). They were extensively rebuilt and repaired in the 1990s, and the c. 1642 timber-framed Rose Cottage, built to house workers on the site, was conserved in 1975. However, immediately to the south lie the restored boring pool and the landscaped remains of the steel furnaces that formed the initial phase of this complicated site. These were built by Sir Basil Brooke around 1619 and were located by the work of the Ironbridge Archaeology Unit in 2001–05. Brook was a prominent industrialist and ironmaster who operated several iron furnaces and forges in the Gorge. By 1786 this industrial complex, by then in the hands of the Dale Company, included the Upper Forge pool, two forges, air furnaces, tenements, and a warehouse. Immediately to the south lay a malthouse and a boring mill with its own pool. The malthouse had been built on the site of the earlier steelworks and itself was adapted for housing in the nineteenth century before being demolished in 1967 (Belford, 2018, 164–165; Belford & Ross, 2004, 215).

Prior to 2001 below-ground archaeological work had been limited. Survey work in the mid-1990s focussed on the standing remains of the eighteenth- and nineteenth-century Upper Forge buildings. This confirmed that the Upper Forge was built in 1776 as a

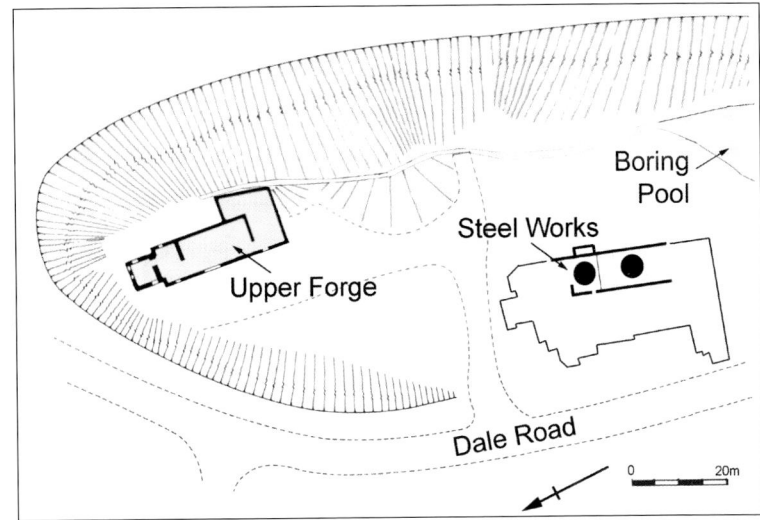

Plan of the location of the seventeenth-century steelworks and Boring Pool at the Upper Forge, Coalbrookdale.

water-powered slitting mill but converted into a forge around 1783. The new brick-built Upper Forge building was used to draw the iron into bars (Hayman, Horton & White, 1999, 39–41). In 1827 the old forge was in use as stables, and by 1838 the Upper Forge had also been turned into a stable block. The engine house was converted into a corn grinding mill, an upper gable and hoist bay being added (Hayman, Horton & White, 1999, 55–57).

Excavations from 2001 to 2005 by the Ironbridge Archaeology Unit focussed on excavating the site of the malthouse, in the process uncovering details of its final use as workers' housing and more surprisingly locating the site of Brook's seventeenth-century steelworks. This work was undertaken as part of the Coalbrookdale Historical Archaeology Research & Training programme, a project that involved university students and volunteers helping to uncover both the domestic and industrial story of this part of Ironbridge (Belford, 2003).

The research showed that the first phase of the site, the initial steel furnace, was built around 1619, and subsequently modified and extended (probably around 1630) when a second furnace was added. The two furnaces were found to have been extensively truncated by the reuse of the site as a malthouse. Nevertheless, enough survived to show that each furnace was circular in form, the earlier northern furnace being 4.57 metres in diameter, before being enlarged in the 1630s to 5.48 metres in diameter, the same size as the southern furnace, added in the later 1630s or early 1640s. These steel furnaces, which were housed in a single-storey building, were similar in plan to later seventeenth-century examples built in Birmingham, Bristol, and Sheffield. Both Upper Forge steel furnaces had two separate ashpits on which a coal fire was lit to heat the cementation chest. Refractory material excavated from the furnaces suggests that they operated at a temperature range of 1,300–1,500 degrees Celsius. The wrought iron in the chest would have been packed with charcoal and the carbon from the charcoal was absorbed into the iron, thus making the steel. The furnaces went out of use in the 1680s (Belford & Ross, 2007).

In the late seventeenth century the site underwent changes in ownership and design, and by the 1730s the steel furnaces had been mostly demolished and the buildings

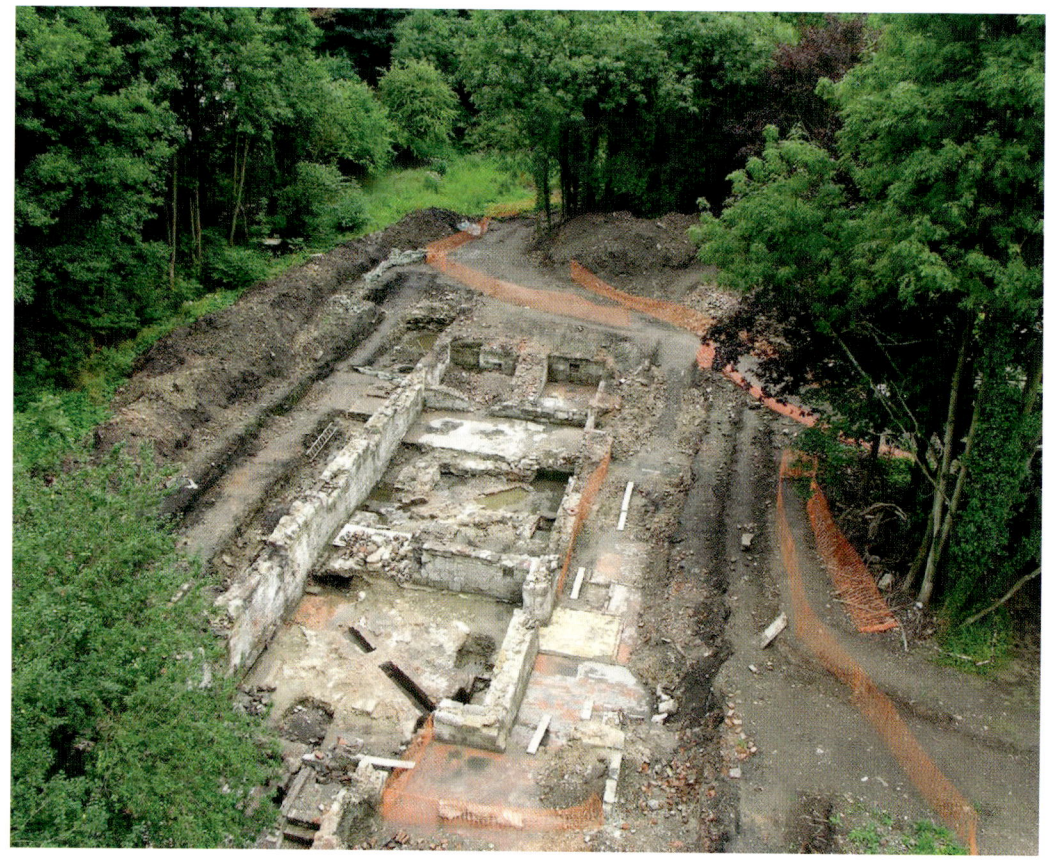

An aerial view of the excavation of the seventeenth-century steelworks and later tenements at the Upper Forge in 2005. (© Ironbridge Gorge Museum Trust)

surrounding it then adapted for use in the malting process (see Dig 8), including the building of a malthouse on the site of the steelworks. The excavations uncovered settling tanks, the base of the drying kiln, and several types of drying floor tiles, from a complex bigger than the surviving malthouse on The Wharfage (Dig 8).

The final phase saw the malthouse converted into tenement housing. Already, by the later eighteenth century a rather ramshackle range of tenements had been added to the western side of the malthouse. In the 1840s the malthouse itself was converted into a row of twelve back-to-back houses. These survived in use until 1967. Excavations in 2002 revealed an old domestic cooking range in one of the kitchens and several fireplaces still in place (Belford & Ross, 2004).

The excavation and documentary work undertaken on the malthouse site in the mid-2000s suggests that the first Upper Forge building was established as part of a new integrated steelworks in the 1610s. Large-scale steel making using the cementation steel process was rare in the seventeenth century and the Upper Forge works appears to have been the first such complex in Britain, further emphasising Ironbridge's wider role as an area of industrial innovation well before Darby's use of coke to fire the old furnace in 1709 (Belford, 2018, 165).

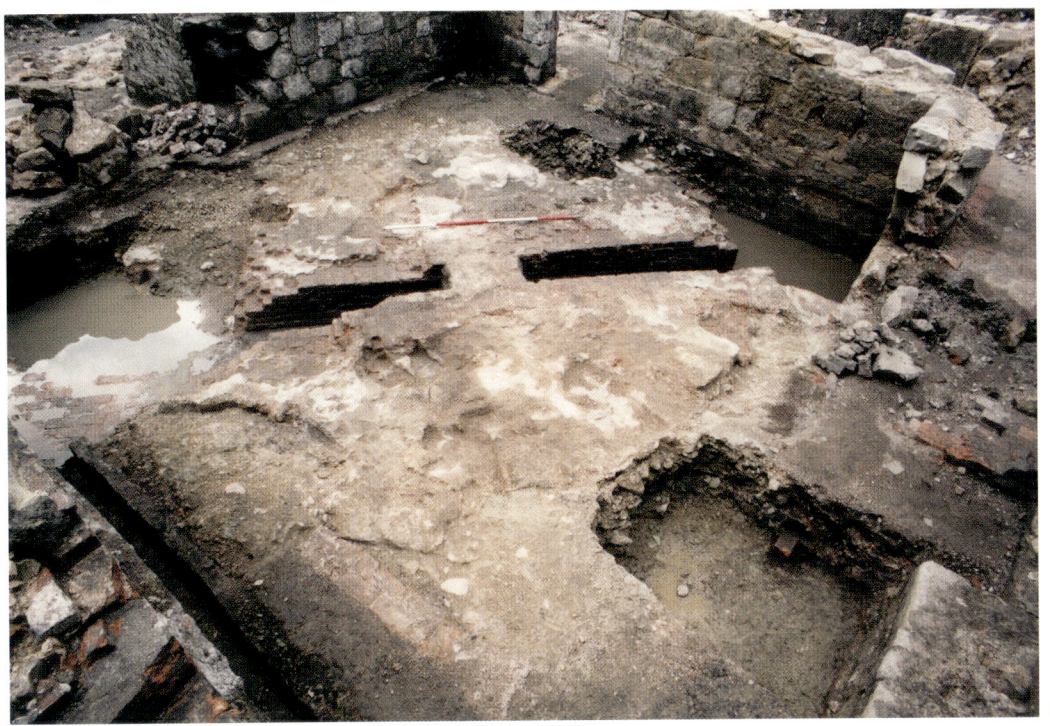

The excavation of the northern, circular-plan, steel furnace in 2005 by Ironbridge archaeologists. (© Ironbridge Gorge Museum Trust)

Dig 17

Coalport Bridge (2004–07)

There were three iron bridges spanning the River Severn in the Gorge. The most famous of these was the innovative first bridge of 1779 (see Dig 20). The Coalport Bridge, which lies east of the Iron Bridge, is the second of these three iron bridges. The last, the Albert Edward Bridge, was built for the Wellington & Severn Junction Railway in 1864. This lies west of the Iron Bridge and about a kilometre upstream from the southern end of Dale Brook, where it meets the River Severn. It still proudly displays a plaque proclaiming the casting of the bridge deck, spans, and parapets by the Coalbrookdale Company.

Coalport Bridge was erected by a turnpike trust to link what would become Coalport on the northern bank of the river with Broseley to the south. Originally called Preens Eddy Bridge but known locally as the Wood Bridge from 1799, the main fabric was timber with stone abutments and a central masonry pier supporting two wooden arches. After the pier was damaged in the great Severn flood of 1795 it was rebuilt in 1799–1800 with a single timber arch and decking carried on three cast-iron ribs. It was rebuilt a second time in 1818 (confirmed by a plaque on the bridge), after the central

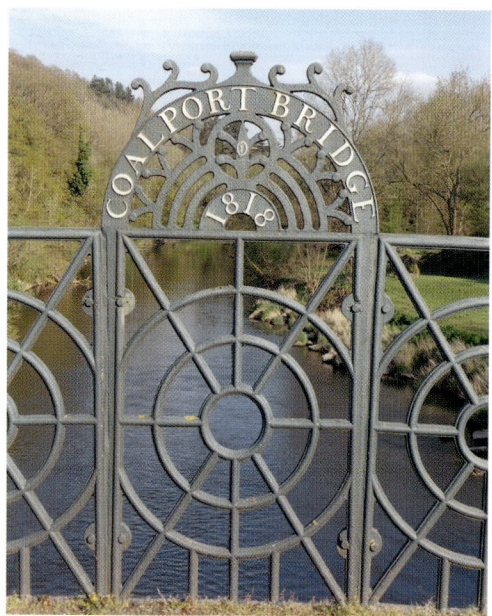

The cast-iron railings on the parapet of the Coalport Bridge commemorating the rebuilding of the bridge using Coalbrookdale iron in 1818.

arch rib fractured. This time, five cast-iron ribs supported a cast-iron deck and parapets. These were manufactured by John Onions & Son of Broseley. The Onions family began their iron business in the mid-eighteenth century and John Onions Sr, described on his death in 1819 as the father of the Shropshire iron trade, was a contemporary of fellow Gorge ironmaster John Wilkinson (Hayman & Horton, 1999, 25–28).

The bridge, which has a single span of 31.4 metres and is 5.5 metres wide, has survived into the twenty-first century with the addition of minor alterations and repairs. An archaeological survey of the structure was undertaken in 1999 ahead of repairs to the bridge abutments. In 2004 Ironbridge Archaeology carried out a small excavation and watching brief at the bridge as part of a project to strengthen and repair a temporary footbridge structure erected over the existing bridge. Four trenches, two each side of the river, were dug for the footings of the temporary bridge, each to a depth of over 5 metres. Whilst only disturbed ground and the natural geology was revealed, pottery recovered from the upper layers of these foundation trenches was dated to the late eighteenth and early nineteenth centuries. One piece was securely dated to the period 1800 to 1814, suggesting there was extensive earth moving and landscaping when the bridge was rebuilt in 1817–18.

In 2007 Ironbridge Archaeology returned to the bridge to undertake further excavation as a result of drainage works at the southern end of the structure. Two narrow (0.5-metre-wide) drainage trenches were dug up to the wall of the bridge but were no more than 0.5 metres deep. Whilst each only encountered disturbed ground from the twentieth century, the sandstone foundations of the southern bridge abutment were located in Trench 2, as was the edge of a stone and concrete retaining wall along the riverbank (Watson, 2007).

Both digs provided detailed information on the depths of redeposited material used in the levelling necessary for the reconstruction of the bridge in 1817–18. They also provided a first glimpse of the structure of the southern abutment foundation and the way in which this part of the structure was built.

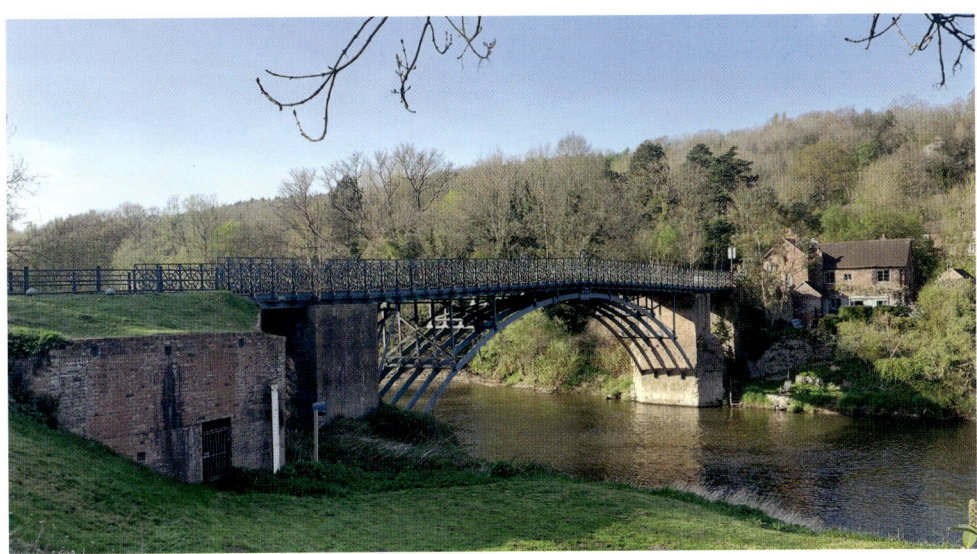

The Coalport Bridge, which lies east of the Iron Bridge, is the second of three iron bridges to span the Gorge. The first bridge erected on this site in 1795 was wood and stone. It was rebuilt partially in iron in 1799–1800, but completely rebuilt in iron in 1818.

Dig 18

The Old Wynd, Shropshire Canal (2014)

The most visible parts of the Shropshire Canal, as it snakes its way down the northern side of the Gorge, are the water-filled stretches at Blists Hill (Dig 5), the Coalport Canal (Dig 13), and the railway known as the Hay Inclined Plane (Dig 3), which linked these two elements. In the early nineteenth century the line of the canal left the Shrewsbury–Newport Canal alignment at Wappenshall, travelling south-eastwards to Wrockwardine Wood, where the Donnington Canal joins it, before turning south towards the River Severn. After several kilometres and just south of the Stirchley Tunnel the canal forks, with the eastern branch heading almost due south towards Blists Hill and Coalport. The western branch, which ran for 4.4 kilometres through Horsehay, may have been intended to reach the Coalbrookdale ironworks, the Coalbrookdale Company being major investors in the canal. However, the line finished close to the top of the Dale at

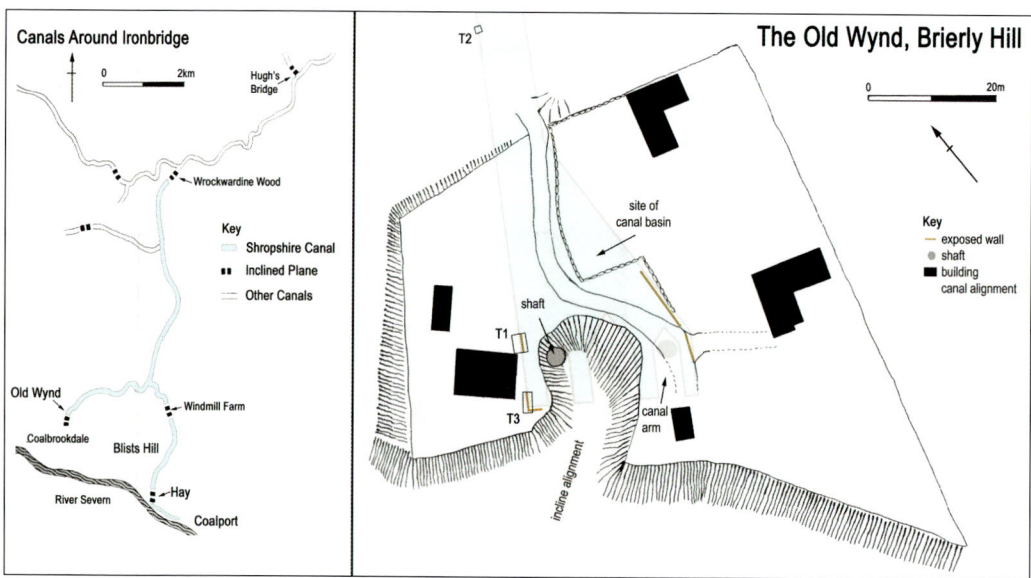

The location of the archaeological work and surviving features at the Old Wynd, a canal basin and transhipment point on the Shropshire Canal at Brierley Hill above Coalbrookdale.

Brierley Hill, 50 metres above the Upper Forge Pool (Hadfield, 1966, 152–159; Hayman & Horton, 1999, 66–67).

Here can be found one of the most curious transport features of the Gorge. At this point the canal ended in a basin and goods were transferred to the plateways in the Dale via an inclined plane that survives today as a long scar up the valley side. However, before this arrangement was opened around 1800, goods were briefly transhipped by a series of tunnels and shafts between the canal and the plateways. This system was built in 1791 and was known as the Old Wynd. The site was first explored by Ironbridge archaeologists from 1983 to 1985, who undertook a landscape survey of the canal basin and recorded a stone-built bridge at its entrance. Formal excavation had to wait until the twenty-first century, when the Ironbridge Archaeology Volunteer Group investigated the canal basin in September 2014 (Beale, 1988; Smith, 2015).

Construction of the Shropshire Canal began in 1788 and by 1791 had reached the site of the Old Wind and the edge of a substantial drop into the Severn Valley. At Brierley Hill two vertical shafts, each 36.6 metres deep and 3 metres wide, were dug. These lay between the three canal arms which formed the southern side of basin. Cranes lowered iron, iron ore, and coal in iron crates down the shafts and raised limestone for use in furnaces further along the canal in Hinkshay. A counter-balance system was used to move the goods, whilst plateways took the loads to and from the bottom of the vertical shafts.

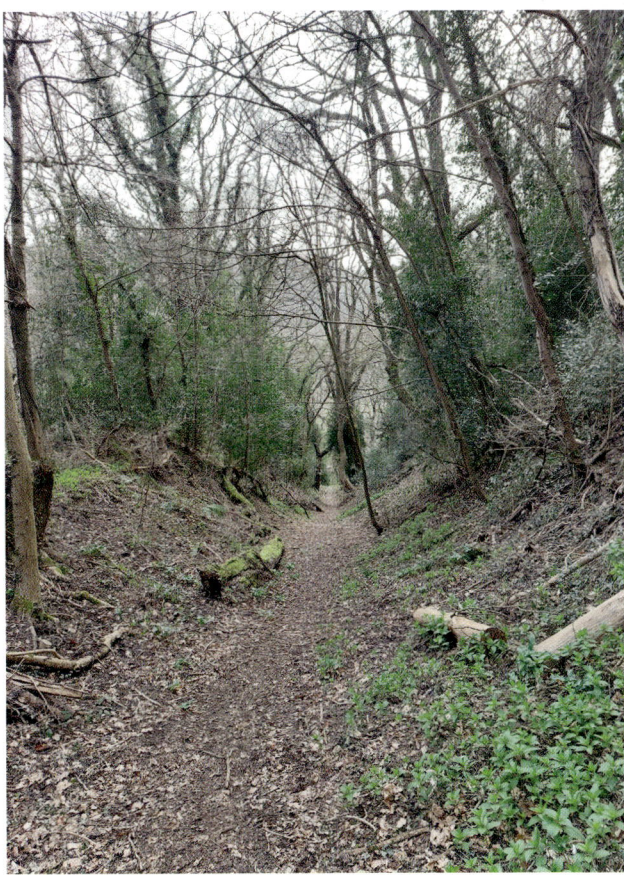

The surviving line of the *c.* 1800 incline linking the Old Wynd canal basin with the Upper Works in the valley below, 2023.

The shaft and tunnels were in operation by July 1791, the construction and management of the system being funded by the Coalbrookdale Company (Hadfield, 1966, 157). Sketches of the winding system and two cranes were made by John Curr and survive in a letter from 1793 (Ironbridge Gorge Museum Library & Archives CBD59.84.3).

Breakdown and transhipment problems seem to have prompted the Coalbrookdale Company to augment the transhipment system with a counterbalanced inclined plane to carry wagons, not boats. This involved filling in the two eastern arms of the canal basin and building a plateway line that ran alongside the remaining western canal arm. From here the line ran along the escarpment edge roughly 150 metres to the east, to the top of an inclined plane, which then ran down the side of the valley for roughly 120 metres to join the existing plateway coming from the lower entrance to the two tunnels. The expanded transhipment complex was opened in September 1794 (Beale, 1988).

The shafts and the inclined plane worked alongside each other until 1800 but the continuing unreliability of the shafts forced their abandonment. In their place a second inclined plane was built, running directly south of the western canal arm down the valley side for 260 metres until it joined the road known as Cherry Tree Hill. A new plateway was built along the canal towpath northwards from the Old Wynd to Horsehay. The eastern incline and the shafts were then closed. The rebuilt canal basin and its second inclined plain continued in use until about 1820 when it was replaced by a plateway running through the Lightmoor valley to the east (Hadfield, 1966, 159; Trinder, 2000).

The 2014 investigation was prompted by the discovery of the top of a vertical brick-lined shaft, the western one of the two original shafts dug in 1791. A horizontal

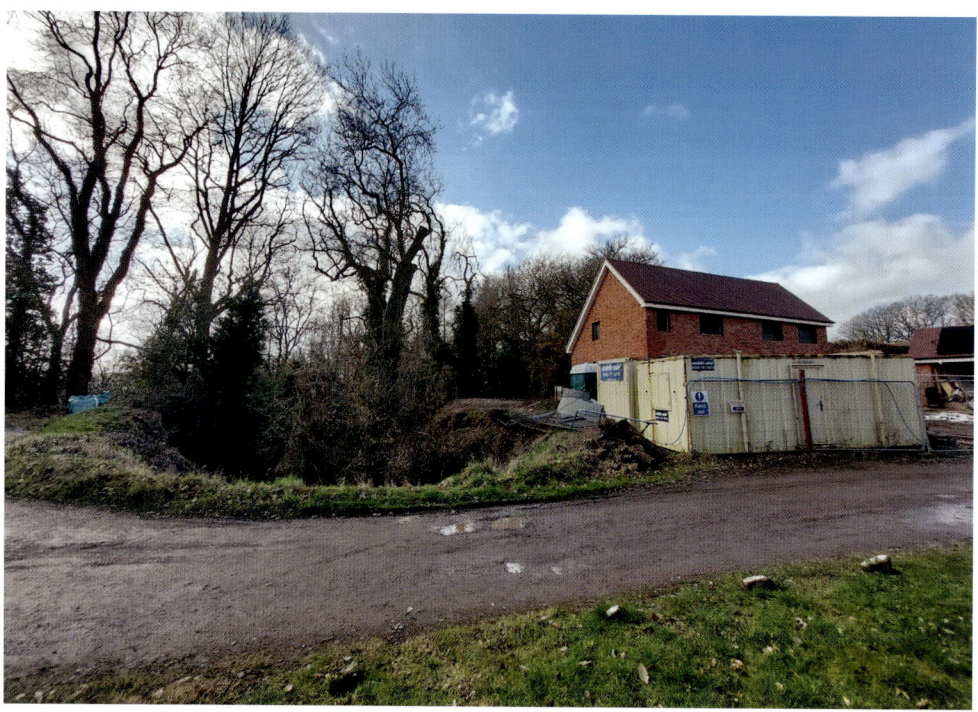

The site of the top of the incline, the wooded area in the centre of the picture, at the Old Wynd, in 2023. The roadway marks the line of the canal.

tunnel was located in 1996 leading under the canal basin towards to the top of the incline, which also appeared to be part of this system. Aside from a few test pits in the mid-1980s, no formal archaeological excavation had been done on the site of the canal basin. The intention of the 2014 project was thus to locate any remains relating to the basin, inclined plain and shafts, and any evidence for improvement carried out on the hoist and shaft system in 1793 (Smith, 2015; Trinder, 2000).

Three small trenches were dug to locate these remains. Trench 1 was positioned over the site of the western wall of the canal basin, the top three stone courses of which was located. The basin appeared to rest on a hard compact layer beneath which was natural clay. Trench 3 was located over the south-western corner of the west dock. Here the top of a 3-metre length of ashlar wall, topped by a stone coping, was uncovered, ending in a 90-degree return at its southern end representing the end of the western canal arm. Trench 2 was located in the bed of the canal to the north of the basin.

These excavations confirmed that substantial canal dock walls remain in situ in good condition. Whilst no evidence was uncovered for the transhipment improvements documented in the letter from 1793, the pottery and glass finds from the three trenches were found to date to the nineteenth and twentieth century, suggesting that the dock remained open for many decades after it was abandoned.

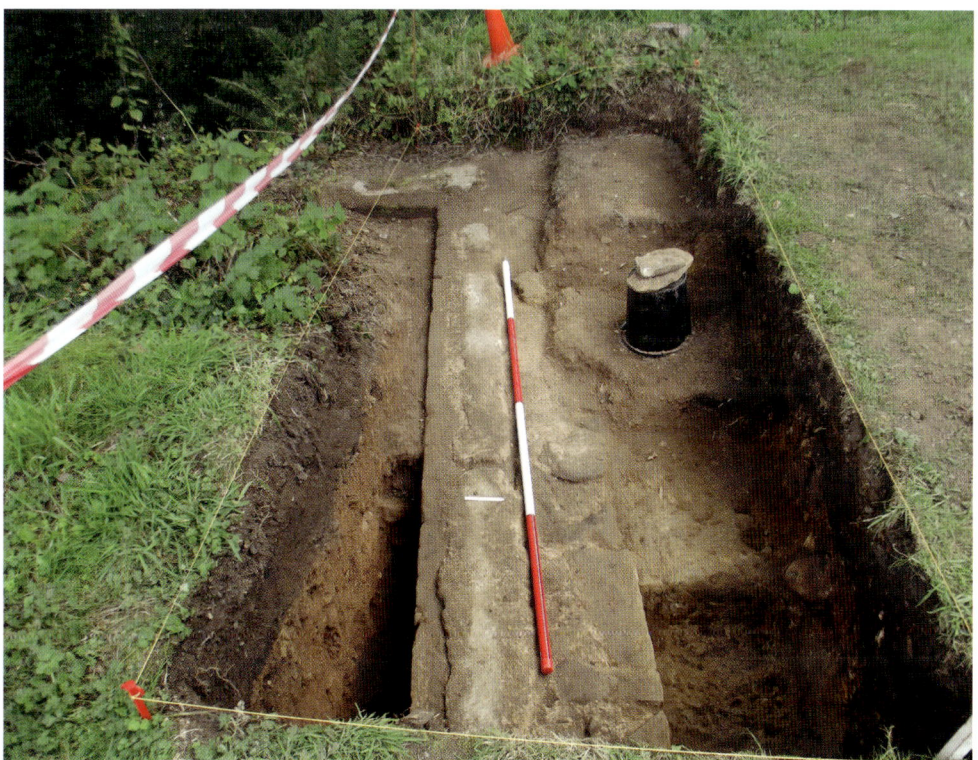

The excavation of T3 in 2014 revealed the south-western corner of one of the original canal arms. This work was undertaken by the Ironbridge Gorge Museum Trust archaeology volunteers. (© Ironbridge Gorge Museum Trust & Ironbridge Gorge Museum Trust archaeology volunteers)

Dig 19

The Lower Forge Dig
(2014–16)

The Lower Forge, one of the five ironworking complexes along the Dale, was the least understood of these sites in terms of its date and history until the twenty-first century (Clark, 1993, 42–45; see Dig 1 and Dig 14). Documentary sources suggested that it was potentially one of the earliest forge sites in Coalbrookdale. In 1536 a 'Newhouse and Calbroke Smithy' were leased to Hugh Morrell. The 'Calbroke Smethe' is mentioned again in 1544 as part of the sale of the manor of Madeley to Robert Brooke, and the suggestion has been made that this early smithy was probably at the site of the later Lower Forge. A cast-iron waterwheel was exposed during building work in the 1880s and around the same time iron hearth plates, some with the date 1602 on them, were

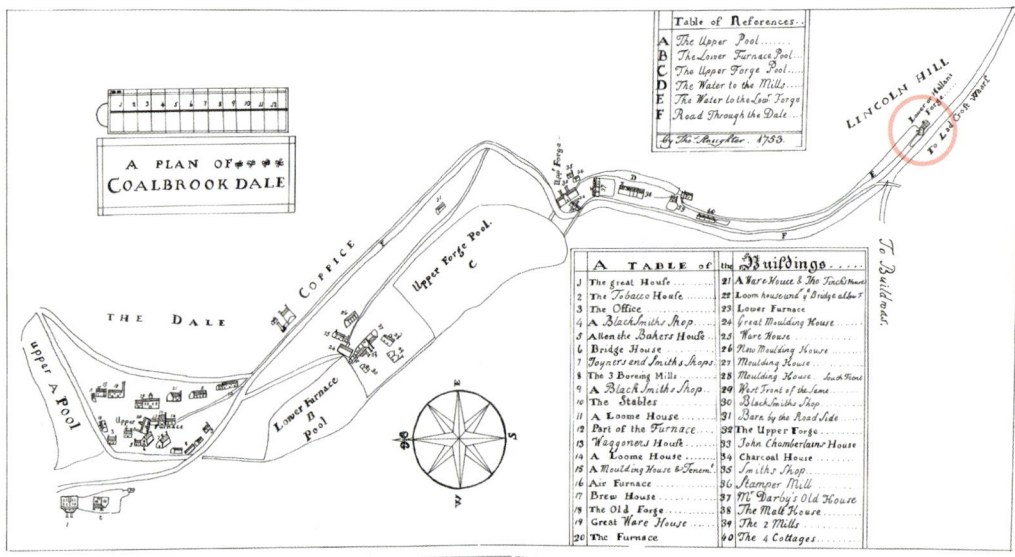

A copy of the 1753 plan of Coalbrookdale by Thomas Slaughter. This plan shows all the major ironworking sites along the Dale Brook – the Upper Furnace, the Lower Furnace, and the Upper Forge – in detail for the first time. It also includes the Lower Forge and its buildings (here circled in red on the right-hand side of the drawing). (© Ironbridge Gorge Museum Trust)

recorded at this site (Baugh, 1985, 48; Belford, 2018, 141; Raistrick, 1953, 54–55). A sixteenth-century origin is further suggested by the site's position, close to where the Dale Brook enters the River Severn. This is the easiest place in the valley to build such a forge, and its pool, since the Dale valley is at its widest at this point (Belford, 2018, 140; Hayman, Horton & White, 1999, 13).

In 1694 the Lower Forge was being used for hammering frying pans from plates of iron. Presumably a waterwheel, or perhaps two waterwheels, were running bellows for the furnace and powering a trip hammer to mould the iron plates. By 1838 this site was in use for nail-making. The forge closed soon after, and by the late nineteenth century most of the forge buildings had been demolished. By this date the site had become a railway depot for the railway accessing the ironworks sites along the Dale and included a warehouse building. The Lower Forge Pool was partly backfilled by 1883 and had completely disappeared by 1901 (Alfrey & Clark, 1986, 36; Clark, 1993, 43, 45).

Little archaeological work had been undertaken on the site before the twenty-first century. The cast-iron waterwheel had been exposed again in 1969, and in 1986 when Ironbridge archaeologists dug a section through the Lower Forge. In 1996 further work in the south-west corner of the site revealed industrial metal deposits 1.5 metres below the current ground service. A decade later in 2006, evaluation work after the demolition of some of the later structures on the site revealed remains relating to eighteenth- and nineteenth-century activity at the Lower Forge, including the substantial western stone wall of the pool dam (Belford, 2018, 140; Trueman, 1986, 56).

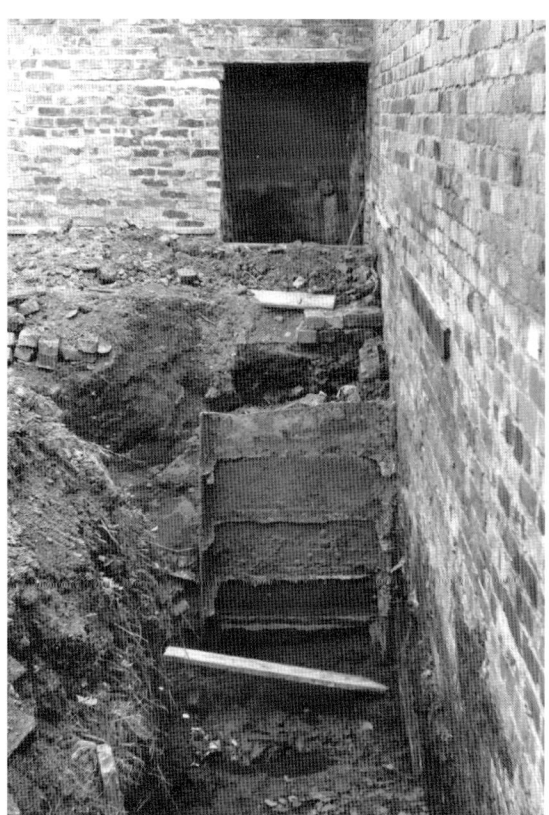

The cast-iron nineteenth-century waterwheel for the Lower Forge as revealed in 1969. (© Ironbridge Gorge Museum Trust)

A proposal for house building led to archaeological work on the site by the Clwyd Powys Archaeological Trust between November 2014 and September 2016. A number of significant structures were exposed relating to the site of the Lower Forge, including the uncovering once more of the cast-iron waterwheel. This waterwheel sat at the south-western corner of the pool and was aligned west to east, with a water-powered grindstone immediately to the northern and a machine base of unclear function to the south. It appeared to be nineteenth century in date, as was its brick-built wheelpit and associated water management features such as leats, sluice, and culverts.

Paul Belford, Ironbridge Archaeology director from 2000 to 2010, has noted that such forge sites could be very long-lived and often reused earlier locations. It thus seems likely that the Lower Forge site probably began in the sixteenth century and is almost certainly the smithy mentioned in documents from 1536 and 1544. This would make it the earliest ironworking site to be so far excavated with the Gorge (Belford, 2018, 137–144; Belford & Ross, 2007, 107).

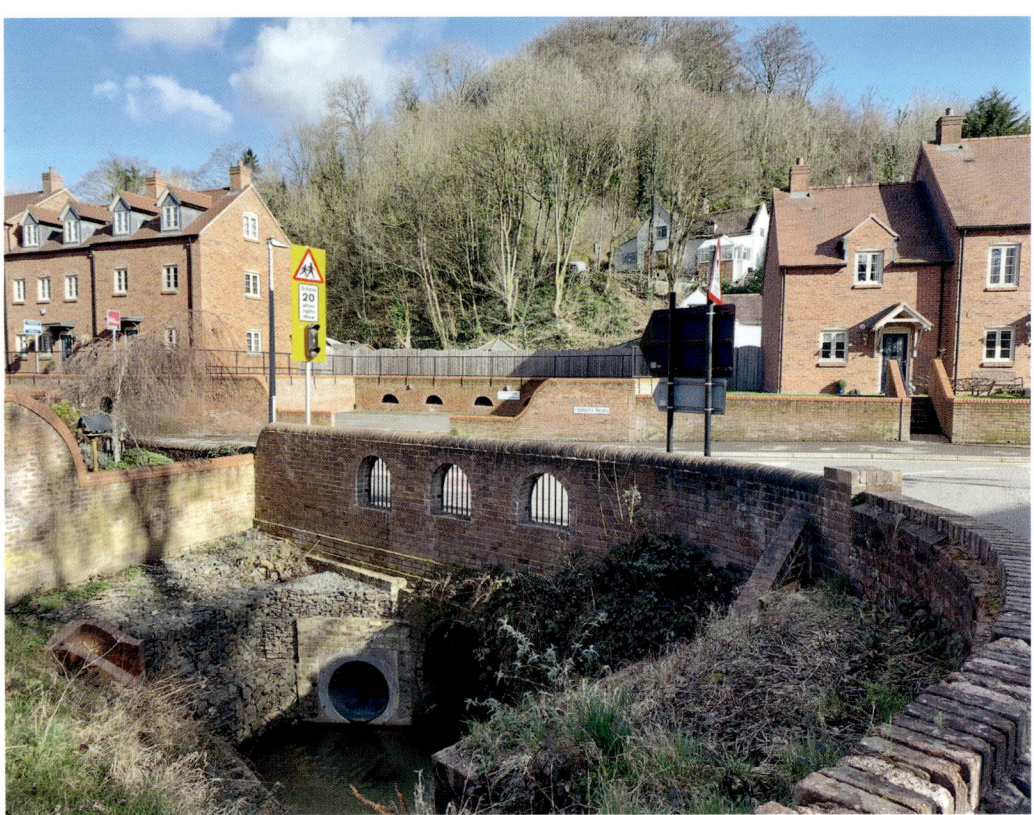

The location of the Lower Forge in 2023. The site of the forge is now occupied by brick-built apartments, with undercrofts designed to cope with frequent flooding, on the far side of Wellington Road. In the foreground the reworked tail race can be seen running south from the forge wheelpit.

Dig 20

Saving the Iron Bridge (1999–2018)

The most visible, and iconic, element of the Ironbridge World Heritage Site is the Iron Bridge. This spans the River Severn in a graceful cast-iron arch, linking Madeley on the northern bank and Broseley on the southern bank. Protected as a Scheduled Monument since 1934, the structure is the world's first cast-iron single-span arched bridge. It has been studied and conserved as a historic monument since the mid-twentieth century, but in the twenty-first century it has also been explored as an industrial archaeological object. These research and preservation strands culminated in the years 2016 to 2018

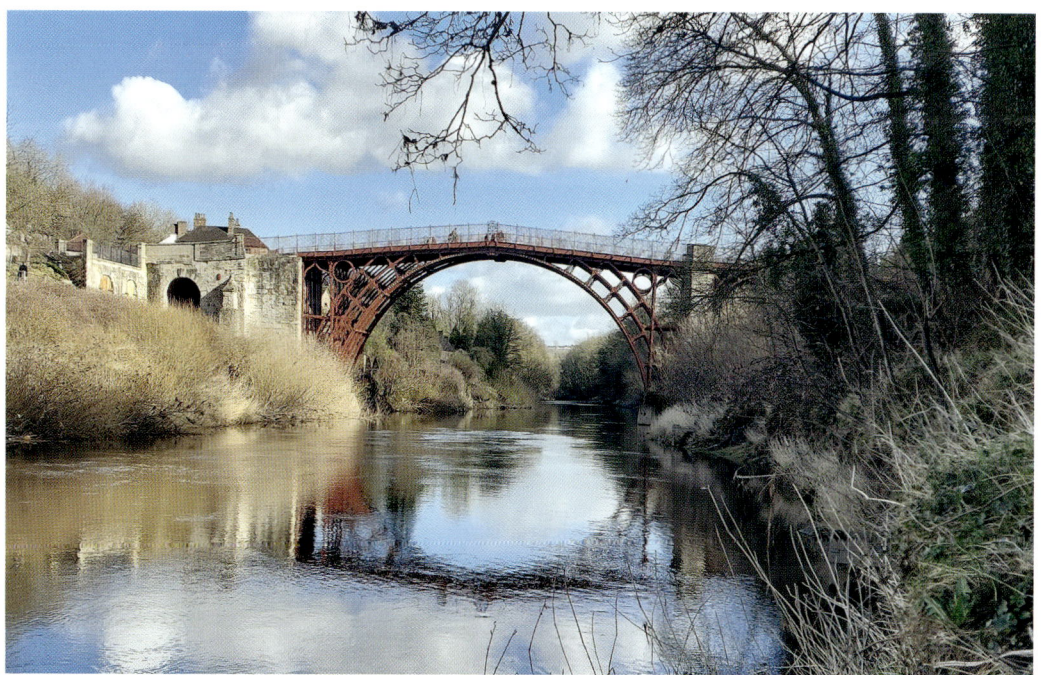

The eastern elevation of the Iron Bridge in 2023. This was the most fashionable vista of the bridge to sketch and paint during the late eighteenth and nineteenth centuries. Its location still captures the drama of an iron structure arching over the deceptively calm waters of the River Severn.

when the English Heritage Trust undertook an extensive programme of conservation, encompassing repair work to the bridge, archaeological survey and limited excavation, and reinterpretation of its construction history.

A series of ferries had linked the northern and southern banks of the River Severn along the 12 kilometres between Buildwas and Bridgnorth since the late medieval period. However, the industrial expansion of the Gorge in the eighteenth century meant that by the 1770s there was a need for a permanent bridge crossing the river to take road traffic between the growing industrial areas of Madeley and Broseley. In 1773, Shrewsbury architect Thomas Pritchard (1723–77) wrote to the ironmaster John Wilkinson suggesting the construction of an iron bridge across the Severn Gorge. After several years of planning, which brought together a range of local sponsors including Abraham Darby III and Wilkinson, an Act of Parliament was approved for the construction of a toll bridge in March 1776, under the name of the 'Severn Bridge at Benthall' (Trinder, 2000, 97–99). Despite the subsequent withdrawal of Wilkinson from the project and the death of Pritchard in 1777, construction went ahead under the direction of Darby.

The site chosen for the bridge was where a ferry crossing owned by Darby linked the wagon roads of Madeley Wood to the north with Broseley to the south. Although the overall design of the bridge was Thomas Pritchard's, Darby and his foreman patternmaker Thomas Gregory undertook the manufacturing of the bridge components and the design of their jointing (Cossons & Trinder, 2002, 23–28; de Haan, 2011, 17–18). The bridge was constructed from 378.5 tons of cast iron and a small amount of wrought iron and spans 100 feet 6 inches (*c.* 30.5 metres) long. The main structure comprises five parallel semicircular ribs, braced laterally to each other, and rising to roughly 50 feet (15.25 metres) above the river. Cast into the two outer ribs are the words 'This Bridge was cast at Coalbrook-Dale and erected in the year MDCCLXXIX'. The spandrels, between the curve of the arch and the abutments, contain iron circles and an ogee-shaped frame, both design features used by Pritchard. The bridge is topped by delicate wrought-iron handrails (de Haan, 2004, 4–5).

The personal account book of Abraham Darby III records expenditure on the Iron Bridge project between the years 1776 and 1781. Three years of design and preparation were needed, involving building the stone bridge foundations and casting the iron parts – the large ones were made at the nearby Bedlam Furnace (Dig 4) and smaller pieces were perhaps made at the rebuilt Old Furnace (Dig 1) (de Haan, 2022). The erection of the bridge itself began in July 1779 when the level of the River Severn was at its lowest. Although the cast-iron framework of the bridge was erected over three months, the roads to the north and south took another two years to complete. The toll bridge finally opened to traffic in January 1781, though there was no tollhouse until 1783. As soon as the bridge was finished it was being celebrated as an incredible engineering feat, not least by the Coalbrookdale Iron Company, which had cast the parts. It has attracted tourists from all over the world to marvel at the graceful iron arch ever since (de Haan, 2004, 4–10; Cossons &Trinder, 2002, 33–34).

Worries over the stability of the bridge's foundations and the southern riverbank emerged early on, with cracks noted in the accommodation arch on the southern bank as early as 1784. After further problems, the two subsidiary arches at the southern end of the bridge were built in timber in 1803–04 and rebuilt in iron in 1821–23. Problems of slippage persisted, with strengthening work undertaken in the 1870s and 1880s. Concerns about the bridge's stability were raised once more in the 1920s, and

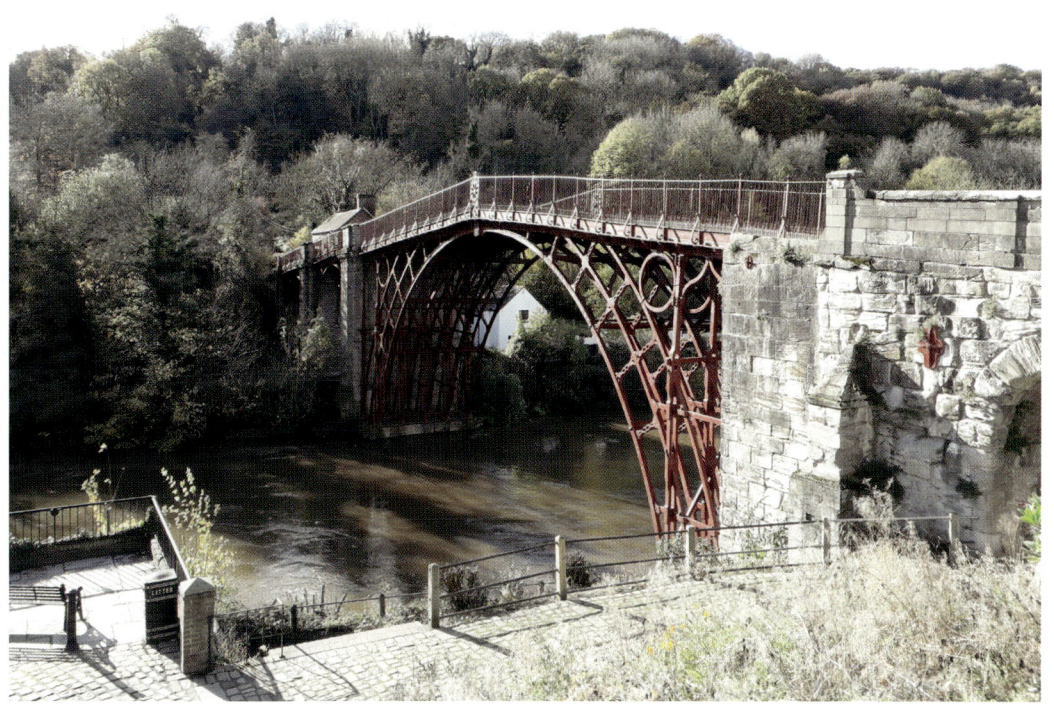

The western elevation of the Iron Bridge in 2020 after the latest conservation work was completed, showing the stone and cast-iron abutments.

in 1923 it was recommended that cement be pumped into the abutments and piers to strengthen them. In an early example of industrial heritage preservation the bridge was designated an Ancient Monument in 1934 and immediately closed to vehicular traffic. The toll for pedestrians was not removed until September 1950 when ownership of the bridge passed to Shropshire County Council. Continued worries about the structure's stability – the abutments had moved 0.48 metres towards each other by 1969 – led to the building in 1972–75 of a concrete strut on the riverbed beneath the bridge bracing the abutments, and to the strengthening of the roadway approach arches on the north bank (de Haan, 2004, 12–14).

Despite being the source of engineering wonder for over 200 years the first complete historic building survey and analysis of the Iron Bridge was not undertaken until 1999 (de Haan, 2000; de Haan, 2004; White 2002a & White 2002b). This was part of restoration work in the years 1999 and 2000 undertaken by English Heritage, by then guardians of the monument. Ironbridge curators and archaeologists conducted a detailed survey treating the bridge as a single structure, rather than a collection of damaged components and subsequent repairs. Examination of the individual structural elements enabled an understanding of the construction phasing and the erection process, with the first rib to be erected being the upstream one. Typological study of the radials suggested that three separate furnaces were used to cast the parts needed. Further work also identified the location of the sandstone quarries used as a source for the northern and southern abutments during the primary construction of the bridge at nearby Ladywood and Hodge Bower (de Haan, 2011; White 2002a, 129–130; Smith, 2020).

In 2006 Ironbridge Archaeology undertook further recording work during repairs to the western, upstream side of the bridge deck surface, which exposed the cast-iron deck plates and the top of the five ribs. This small-scale recording noted differences in the style of casting between the support structs and the main cast-iron ribs (Kelleher, 2016).

Conservation works by English Heritage from 2016 to 2018 involved the grit blasting of the entire iron structure prior to repainting, replacement of failed cast-iron parts, installation of a new road surface, and repairs to the masonry structure of the bridge. The erection of scaffolding around the bridge, as in 1999–2000, allowed further archaeological work to augment the drawings made during the last time the bridge was

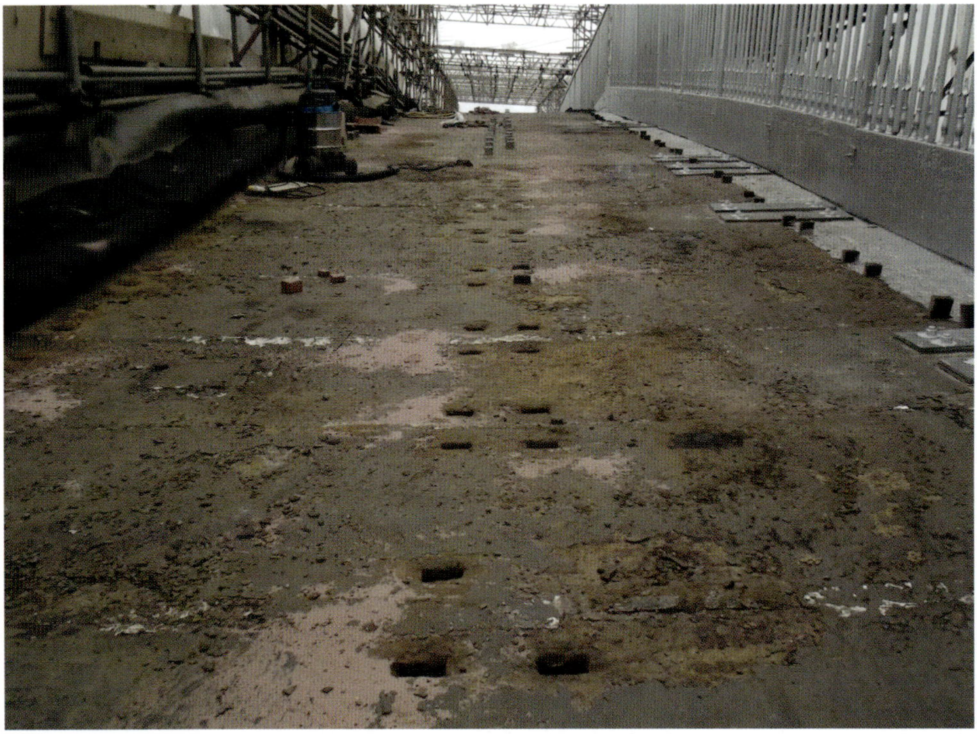

The decking of the Iron Bridge as exposed during conservation and repair works in 2006. (© Ironbridge Gorge Museum Trust)

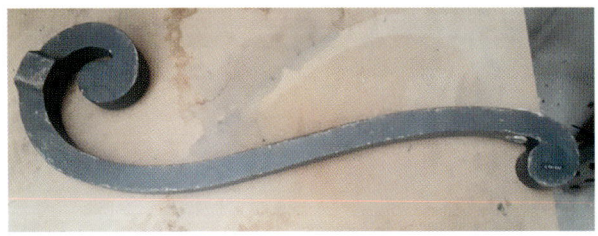

One of the spandrels removed from the Iron Bridge during conservation works in the period 2016–18, and now in the Ironbridge Gorge Museum Trust store.

scaffolded. This confirmed the conclusions of the earlier survey in terms of phasing and provided details of historic repairs to individual structural elements, whilst also providing evidence for the design of the bridge-decking. It also allowed the structure of the road deck to be recorded in detail (Kelleher, 2016; Smith, 2020). The most dramatic element of the restoration work from 2016 to 2018 was the decision to repaint the bridge in red-brown rather than black. This was based upon evidence for this being the primary paint used on the cast-iron beams.

The conservation and reinterpretation of the Iron Bridge in the twenty-first century demonstrates the way in which archaeological analysis of such a well-known industrial heritage structure continues to evolve. This is also true for the other nineteen industrial archaeology monuments within the Ironbridge World Heritage Site which have been explored in this book. Beyond these, there are more than 100 digs, building surveys, and landscape surveys which have been undertaken in and around the Gorge since the Ironbridge Gorge Museum Trust was established in 1968. This makes the valley one of the most intensively studied industrial archaeology landscapes in the world.

Together, this new data has broadened our understanding of the role of the iron, coal, and pottery industries in Ironbridge, and changed our perception of their impact

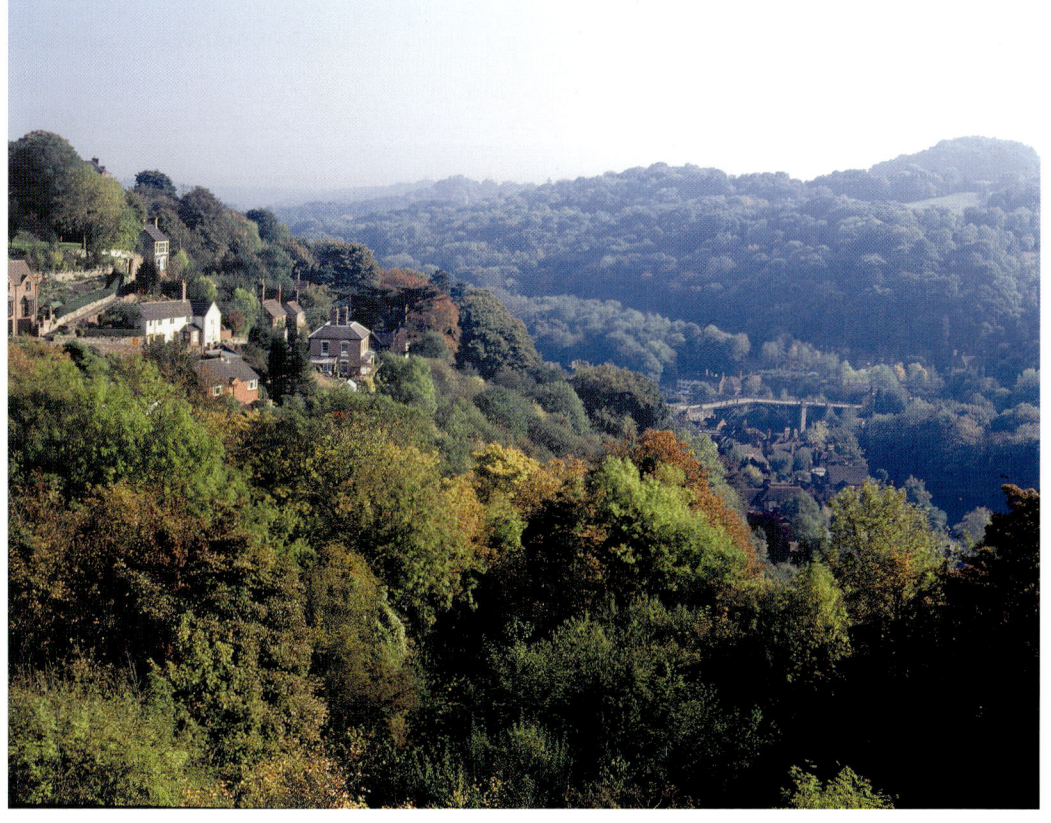

An early twenty-first-century view of the Iron Bridge from the Rotunda at the top of Lincoln Hill. The Ironbridge landscape has long combined the innovation and shock of industry with its impact on the natural landscape. (© Ironbridge Gorge Museum Trust)

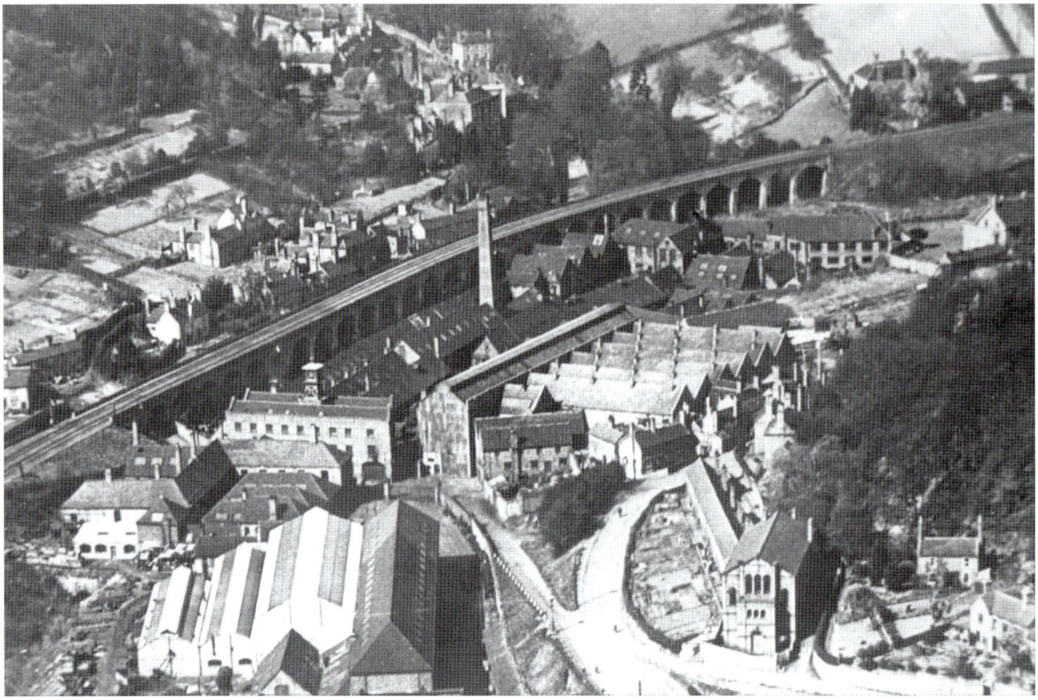

An aerial view of the Upper Works at Colabrookdale in the 1920s showing the buildings between the Great Warehouse, the Long Warehouse, and the railway arches before demolition. (© Ironbridge Gorge Museum Trust)

nationally and globally during the seventeenth, eighteenth, and nineteenth centuries, allowing us to see Ironbridge as one of the first industrialised societies in the world. Its legacy can be seen in the spread of industrialisation led by coal extraction and iron production around the globe during the nineteenth and twentieth centuries. It can also be seen in the conservation and interpretation of the manufacturing sites of the Industrial Revolution in many other countries. As Charles Hulbert (cotton manufacturer, book seller, and writer) observed in 1836, the river valley of the Severn as it flows through the Ironbridge Gorge remains 'the most extraordinary district in the world'.

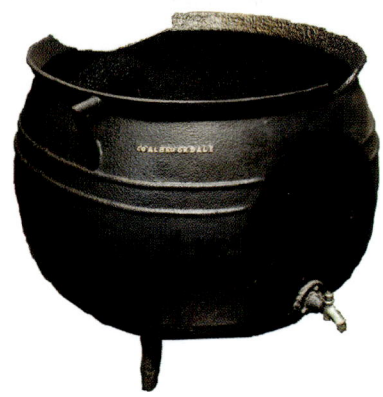

Cast-iron pots manufactured at Coalbrookdale, like this example on display in the Museum of Iron, were exported from Ironbridge to all parts of the world during the eighteenth and nineteenth centuries.

Bibliography

Baggs, A. P., Cox, D. C., McFall, Jessie, Stamper, P. A., & Winchester, A. J. L., 1985, 'Telford', in *A History of the County of Shropshire: Volume 11, Telford, Wenlock Liberty and Borough Continued: Madeley (including Coalbrookdale, Coalport and Ironbridge), Little Wenlock*, ed. G. C. Baugh & C. R. Elrington: London, 1–19.

Baggs, A. P., Baugh, G. C., Cox, D. C., McFall, Jessie, & Stamper P. A., 1998, 'Broseley', in *A History of the County of Shropshire: Volume 10, Munslow Hundred (Part), the Liberty and Borough of Wenlock*, ed. G C Baugh: London, 257–93.

Barker, D. & Horton, W., 1999, 'The development of the Coalport Chinaworks: analysis of ceramic finds', *Post-Medieval Archaeology 33*, 3–93.

Baugh, G. C., (ed.), 1985, *The Victoria County History of the Counties of England: A History of Shropshire, Vol IX* (London: University of London Institute of Historical Research).

Beal, R., 1988, *The Old Wind. A Preliminary Report.* Ironbridge Archaeological Series No. 21.

Belford, P., 2003, 'Forging Ahead in Coalbrookdale: Historical Archaeology at the Upper Forge', *Industrial Archaeology Review 25.1*, 59–63.

Belford, .P, 2007, 'Sublime Cascades: Water and Power in Coalbrookdale', *Industrial Archaeology Review 29.2*, 133–48.

Belford P, 2009a, *Archaeological Investigations at the Darby Furnace Coalbrookdale, Shropshire.* Ironbridge Archaeological Series No. 310.

Belford, P., 2009b, *Archaeological Investigation and Historic Building Recording at Jackfield Tile Museum, Shropshire.* Ironbridge Archaeological Series No. 190.

Belford, P., 2009c, *Archaeological Investigation and Historic Building Recording Coalbrookdale Project, Coalbrookdale, Shropshire.* Ironbridge Archaeological Series No. 135.

Belford, P., 2010a, 'Projects ongoing: reflections on archaeology and industrial heritage in the Ironbridge Gorge', in Belford, Palmer & White, 169–188.

Belford, P. 2010b, *Archaeological Excavations at Double Row, Hinkshay, Telford Town Park.* Ironbridge Archaeological Series No. 307, unpublished report by the Ironbridge Gorge Museum Trust for Telford and Wrekin Council.

Belford, P., 2011, 'Archaeology, Community, and Identity in an English New Town', *The Historic Environment Policy & Practice*, Vol 2.1, 49–67.

Belford, P., 2018, *Blood, Faith and Iron. A Dynasty of Catholic Industrialists in Sixteenth- and Seventeenth-century England.* Oxford: Archaeopress Publishing Ltd.

Belford, P., Palmer, M. & White, R. (eds), 2010, *Footprints of Industry. Papers from the 300th anniversary conference at Coalbrookdale, 3–7 June 2009.* Oxford: Archaeopress, BAR British Series 523.

Belford, P., & Ross, R. A., 2004, 'Industry and Domesticity: Exploring Historical Archaeology in the Ironbridge Gorge', *Post-Medieval Archaeology* 38.2, 215–225.

Belford, P., & Ross, R. A., 2007, 'English steelmaking in the seventeenth century: excavation of two cementation furnaces at Coalbrookdale', *Historical Metallurgy* 41.2, 105–123.

Brown, I., 1979, 'Underground in the Ironbridge Gorge;' *Industrial Archaeology Review* 3.2, 158–169.

Brown, I., 1991, 'The Lloyds, Ironbridge, Shropshire', *Industrial Archaeology Review* 14.1, 5–16.

Clark, C., 1993, *English Heritage Book of Ironbridge Gorge.* London: B. T. Batsford Ltd & English Heritage.

Clark, C., & Alfrey, J., 1986, *Coalport and Blists Hill. Nuffield Survey Second Interim report.* Ironbridge Gorge Museum Trust Research Paper No 14.

Clark, C., & Alfrey, J., 1993, *Landscape of Industry: Patterns of Change in the Ironbridge Gorge.* London and New York: Routledge.

Cossons, N. & Trinder, B., 2002, *The Iron Bridge. Symbol of the Industrial Revolution.* Chichester: Phillimore & Co. Ltd, Second Edition.

de Haan, D., 2000, *The Iron Bridge, Historic Building Survey, Record & Analysis, for English Heritage.* IGMT.

de Haan, D., 2004, 'The Rolt Memorial Lecture 2003. The Iron Bridge – New research in the Ironbridge Gorge', *Industrial Archaeology Review 26.1,* 3–20.

de Haan D., 2011, *Conservation Plan for the Iron Bridge, Ironbridge, Shropshire.* Ironbridge Gorge Museum Trust technical report.

de Haan, D., 2022, *The Story of the Iron Bridge.* IGMT technical report.

Darby, M., 2010, 'Ironworks to Museum: Coalbrookdale 1709-2009', in Belford, Palmer & White, 3–15.

Edmundson, R. S., 1979, 'Coalport China Works, Shropshire: A Comparative Study of the Premises and the background to their development', *Industrial Archaeology Review 3.2,* 122–45.

George, D. & Nevell, M., 2014, 'Revisiting the Iconic: the Excavation of the Reel Fitz Pit Engine and the Newcomen Steam engine in Cumberland, UK', *Industrial Archaeology Review 36.2,* 128–140.

Grant, G., & Crumpton, G., 2020, 'Schooling Good taste: The Coalbrookdale School of Art 1856–1924', *Journal of the Tiles & Architectural Ceramics Society*, volume 26, 1–11.

Griffin, E., 2018, *A Short History of the British Industrial Revolution.* London: Palgrave, Second Edition.

Hadfield, C., 1966, *The Canals of the West Midlands.* Newton Abbot: David & Charles.

Hayman, R., 1997, 'Lloyds Engine house, Ironbridge', *Transactions of the Shropshire Archaeological and Historical Society LXXII,* 38–51.

Hayman, R., and Horton, W., 1996, *The Coalbrookdale Project (Northern Lights). An Archaeological Evaluation.* Ironbridge Archaeology Series No. 65.

Hayman, R., and Horton, W., 1999, *Ironbridge. History and Guide.* Stroud: Tempus Publishing.

Hayman, R., Horton, W. & White, S., 1999, *Archaeology and Conservation in Ironbridge.* York: Council for British Archaeology research report 123.

Hayman, R., & White, S., 1995, *The Coalbrookdale Foundry. A Desk Top Evaluation.* Ironbridge Archaeology Series No. 53.

Higgins, D. A., 1987, *The Interpretation and Regional Study of Clay Tobacco Pipes: a Case Study of the Broseley District.* University of Liverpool PhD thesis.

Higgins, D., Morriss, R., & Trueman, M., 1988, *The Broseley Pipeworks: An Archaeological and Historical Evaluation.* The Ironbridge Gorge Museum Research Paper No. 27.

Horton, M., Clark, C., Trinder, B., & Cox, N., 1992, *Newdale: An Industrial Township of the Mid-eighteenth Century.* A Report on the Archaeological Investigations. Ironbridge Archaeology Series 29.

Horton, W. (ed.), 1997, *Broseley Pipeworks. Final Report.* Ironbridge Archaeological Series No. 71.

Horton, W., Richardson, S., White, S. & Worthington, M., 1993, *Coalport Chinaworks. A Site Investigation for English Heritage.* The Ironbridge Gorge Museum, Severn Gorge Repair Project Report No. 2.

Horton, W., Richardson, S., Sherratt, M., White, S. & Worthington, M., 1993, *The Blists Hill Canal, Hay Inclined Plane and the Coalport Canal. A Site Investigation for English Heritage.* The Ironbridge Gorge Museum, Severn Gorge Repair Project Report No. 3.

Jones, N. W., 1987, 'A Wooden Waggon Way at Bedlam Furnace, Ironbridge', *Post-Medieval Archaeology* 21, 259–62.

Kelleher, S., 2016, *Archaeological Watching Brief During Investigative Works at the Iron Bridge, Ironbridge, Shropshire.* Ironbridge Archaeology Technical Report No. 342.

Leese, J. S., 1912, 'Old English Power Plants', *Power* (New York), 23 July.

Newman, J. & Pevsner, N., 2006, *The Buildings of England: Shropshire.* New Haven & London: Yale University Press.

Page-Smith, K., 2010, *Telford Town Park, Parks for People Project: Archaeological and Historical Desk-based Assessment.* Nexus Heritage, Report No. 3035. Unpublished client report for Telford & Wrekin Council.

Palmer, M., Nevell, M. & Sissons, M., 2012, *Industrial Archaeology: A Handbook.* York: Council for British Archaeology practical handbook No. 21.

Raistrick, A., 1953, *Dynasty of Iron Founders: The Darbys and Coalbrookdale* (revised 1989). Coalbrookdale: Ironbridge Gorge Museum Trust/Sessions Book Trust.

Smith, A., 2015, *Ironbridge Archaeology Volunteer Group Excavation at the Old Wynd, Coalbrookdale.* IAVG Report No. 2.

Smith, S. G., 2020, *The Iron Bridge, Ironbridge. Final Report on Archaeological Recording During the Project Iron Bridge Conservation Works, 2017–8.* Ironbridge Archaeological Series No. 343.

Terry, R., 1988, *The Swan Malthouse, Ironbridge. A Building Survey.* Ironbridge Archaeology Series 22.

Thomas, E., 2001, *Coalbrookdale in the eighteenth Century.* IGMT technical report.

Trinder, B., 2000, *The Industrial Revolution in Shropshire. Third Edition.* Chichester: Phillimore.

Trinder, B., 2008, 'Williams Reynolds Polymath – A Biographical Strand Through the Industrial Revolution', *Industrial Archaeology Review* 30.1, 17–32.

Trinder, B., 2016, *The Industrial Archaeology of Shropshire. Second Edition.* Little Logaston: Logaston Press.

Trinder, B., 2017, *'The Most Extraordinary District in the World'. Ironbridge and Coalbrookdale. An anthology of visitors' impressions of Ironbridge, Coalbrookdale and the Shropshire Coalfield.* Third Edition, revised. Stroud: History Press.

Trueman, M., (ed.), 1986, *Archaeology in Ironbridge 1985–86.* Coalbrookdale: Ironbridge Gorge Museum Trust.

Trueman, M., (ed.), 1988, *Archaeology in Ironbridge 1981–85.* Coalbrookdale: Ironbridge Gorge Museum Trust.

Trueman, M., Jones, A., & MacLeod, M., 1988, *The Upper Works, Coalbrookdale. A Rescue Excavation.* Ironbridge Archaeology Series 13.

Watson, S., 2007, *Excavation and Watching Brief, Coalport Bridge, Shropshire.* Ironbridge Archaeology Series 208.

White, S., 2002a, *The Iron Bridge: Survey, Record and Analysis.* Ironbridge Archaeology, Coalbrookdale technical report No. 100.

White, S., 2002b, *The Iron Bridge: Railing Survey, Record and Analysis.* Ironbridge Archaeology technical report No. 110.

Williams, R., 2017a, 'The performance of Abraham Darby's coke furnace revisited, part 1: temperature of operation', *Historical Metallurgy* 51 (1), 22–33.

Williams, R., 2017b, 'The performance of Abraham Darby's coke furnace revisited, part 2: output and efficiency', *Historical Metallurgy* 51 (2), 87–98.

Winkworth, A., 1988, *23 The Wharfage, Ironbridge.* Ironbridge Archaeological Series No. 16.

Worthington, M., 1993, *Investigation of Blists Hill Wharf Mines: an archaeological desk study and excavation.* Ironbridge Archaeology Series.

Selected Ironbridge Archaeology Archives held at IGMT
C5-15: Blists Hill Blast Furnaces
D21-37: Blists Hill Canal, Mine & Hay Inclined Plane
G1-54: Jackfield
G100-149: Coalport
G240-325: Broseley
G525-39: Ironbridge
G673-82: Bedlam Furnaces

Acknowledgements

I would like to thank the following people and organisations who have helped to explore Ironbridge's archaeology over the last sixty years. Firstly, the staff of the former Ironbridge Gorge Museum Trust Archaeology Unit (also known as Ironbridge Archaeology), based at the museum and led by John Malam, David Higgins, Kate Clark, Wendy Horton, and Paul Belford between 1981 and 2010, and the Ironbridge Archaeologists Shane Kelleher (2010–18) and Spencer Gavin-Smith (2018–21). Secondly, the Director of the Ironbridge Institute, David de Haan, who acted as historical adviser on the Iron Bridge to English Heritage from 1999 to 2012. The fieldwork they oversaw forms the core of this book. My colleagues in the Collections and Learning Department at the Ironbridge Gorge Museum Trust, especially Nick Booth, Kate Cadman, Gillian Crumpton, Sarah Roberts, and Joanne Smith, for advice, cake, and access to materials, reports, and images covering the Gorge's history. I would also like to acknowledge the work of past students from the former Ironbridge Institute for their pioneering industrial archaeology studies on many of the sites across the Gorge included in this volume. Since 2000 an increasing number of archaeological contractors, such as CPAT and Nexus, have undertaken archaeological and historical work that continues to uncover and aide our understanding of the World Heritage Site's archaeological past. I would also like to thank Steve Dewhurst and David de Haan for their immensely helpful comments on a draft version of the manuscript, Kate Clark for advice on the details of several sites, the members of the IGMT archaeology volunteers' group and the Broseley Local History Society for access to their fieldwork, and Michael S. Darby for the use of images of the Old Furnace from his personal collection. Copies of the technical reports researched and written by the Ironbridge Gorge Museum Trust Archaeology Unit can be found in the IGMT Archives, in the Long Warehouse. Copyright attributions and permissions can be found with the relevant images. All other images were taken by the author.

About the Author

Dr Michael Nevell, DPhil, MCIfA, FSA, is the Industrial Heritage Support Officer for England, based at the Ironbridge Gorge Museum Trust. He is an industrial and landscape archaeologist with more than thirty years' experience. His research interests include the archaeology of industrialisation, community archaeology, historic buildings (especially textile mills), timber buildings, and weavers' cottages. Dr Nevell has written extensively on industrial archaeology subjects with books on industrial Glasgow and Manchester. He is co-author of the Council for British Archaeology's *Industrial Archaeology: A Handbook* (2012) and is co-editor of the *Oxford Handbook of Industrial Archaeology* (2022). He was a senior lecturer in archaeology at both the University of Manchester and University of Salford, director of the University of Manchester Archaeological Unit from 2002 to 2009 and founding Head of the Centre for Applied Archaeology at the University of Salford from 2009 to 2020. You can follow him on social media @archaeology_tea and @IHSO England or read his blog: www.archaeologytea. wordpress.com.